Haunted Safari

Jonathan Burrello

a Big Insane Happy production

Haunted Safari
Jonathan Burrello

Published by KDP

*Except for the drawing of Susan Tyrell as the Queen of the Sixth Dimension from the 1980 Oingo Boingo film "The Forbidden Zone" on page 52. That was quite intentional on my part.

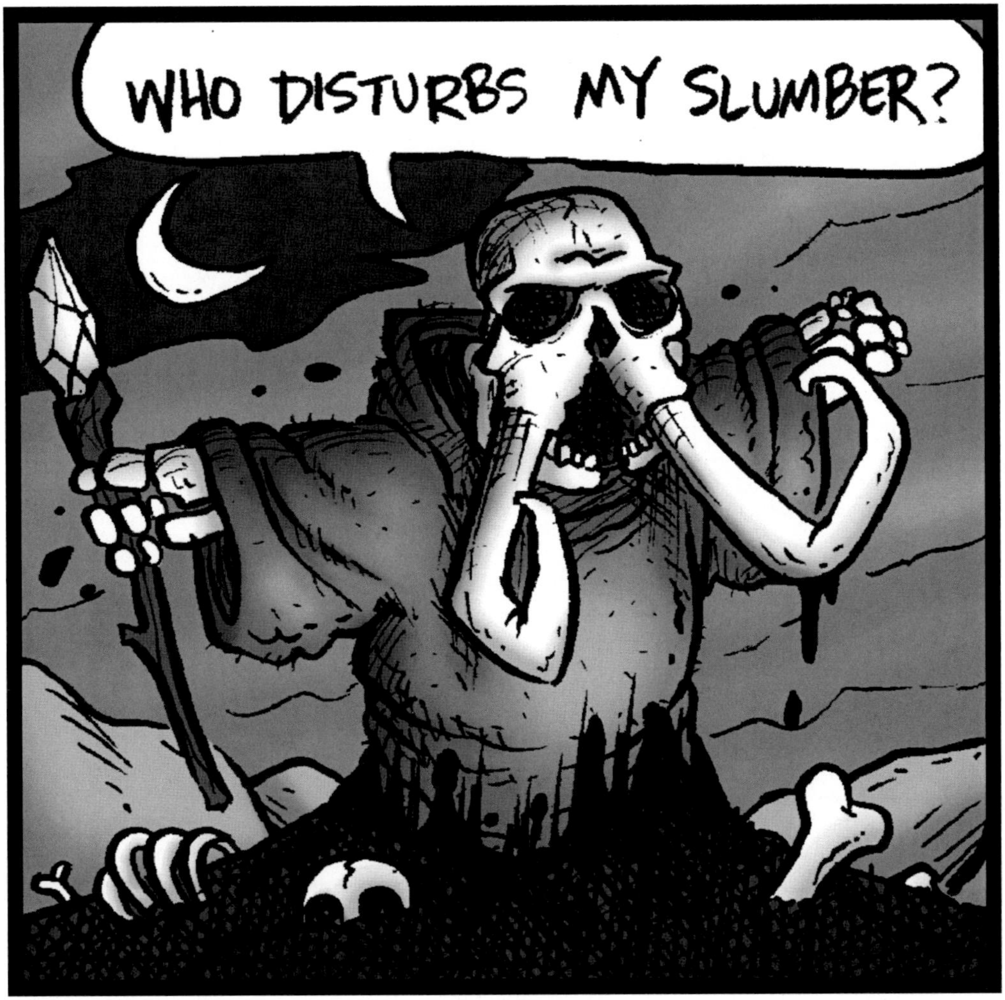
WHO DISTURBS MY SLUMBER?

Like, legit a funny comic book! In addition to appreciating the gorgeous illustrations of whacky little characters — each of whom is just whimsical and strange in a great way — there's wonderful humour and commentary in this collection. It's everything you want in a humour comic strip!

- Rebecca Crunden (*Indie Book Spotlight*)

I loved this comic! I laughed out loud. Just read and enjoy. It has some nice messages about life mixed in too.

-Lucy @lucyturnspages

Haunted Safari is one of those rare gems that comfortably straddles the strata of satire. Not only does Jon make delightfully memorable characters, but he has a true gift for expression.

- Michelle Franklin (*Werewolves Don't Celebrate Hanukkah*)

For wizards, ghosts, bees,
and everyone in between.

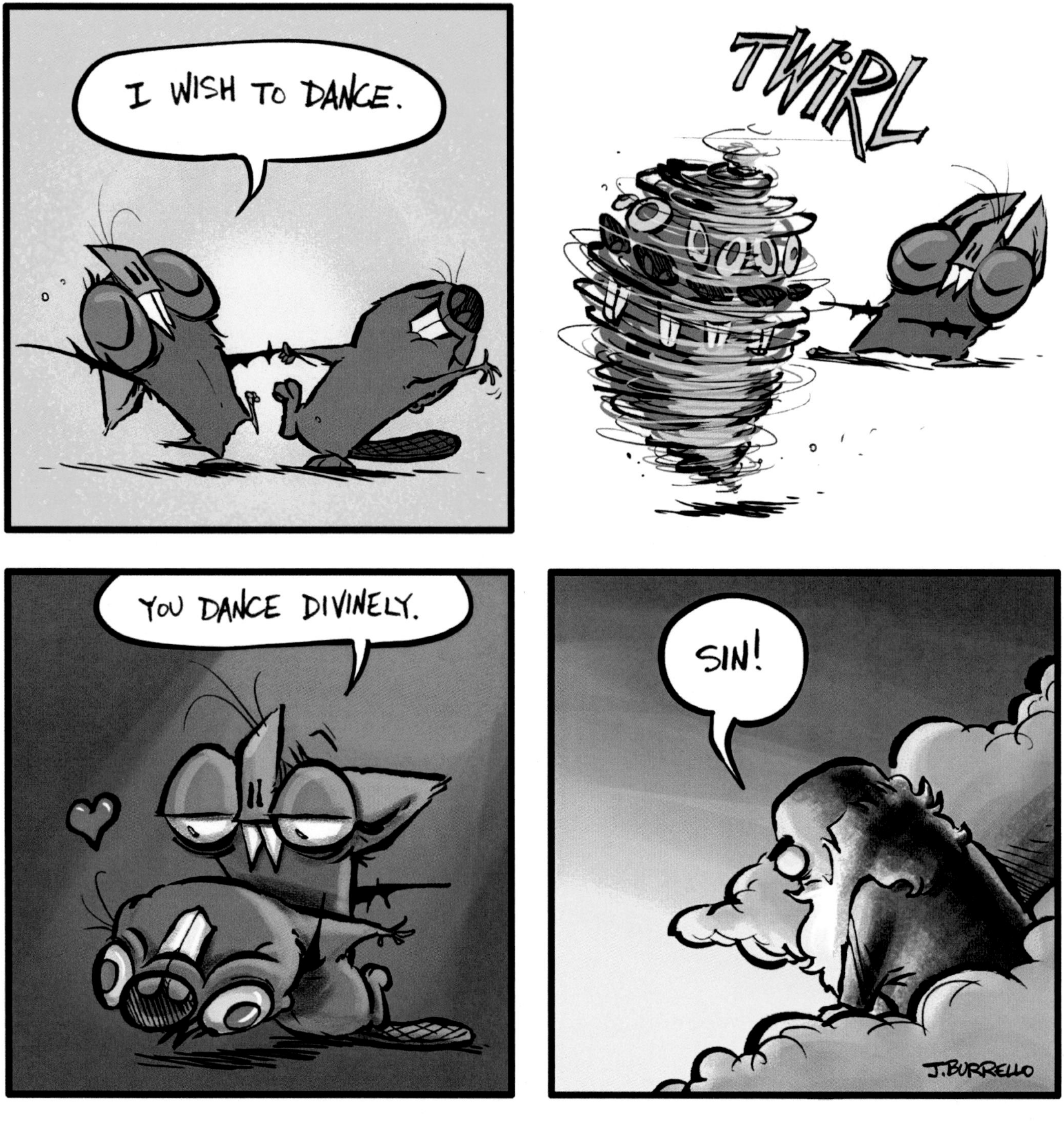
I WISH TO DANCE.
TWIRL
YOU DANCE DIVINELY.
SIN!
J. BURRELLO

I hope you like bats.

Once upon a time, many years ago and after a particularly odd day, I muttered to myself: life is a haunted safari.

I never really knew what that meant, but it sounded right.

Welcome to *Haunted Safari* (previously known as *Blinky & Sal*). Here you will discover my weird little cartoon realm full of gods, monsters, bats, beavers, depressed narwhals, cranky hole-dwellers, and other such inky, crusty critters. That's how we like it around here anyhow.

I think I've given up thinking comics always supposed to "be funny" or "make sense". My favorite comics to read and to write are often more of a vibe than anything else. I reckon that's about what we got here. Hopefully, these pages contain some weirdness and silliness in 'em to tickle ya in a mostly appropriate way.

Everyone's got some weirdness and silliness in 'em. I think it's quite human. Maybe even animal. We're told we must be motivated and industrious. However, I suspect the realest songs of our hearts are far too personal to sound like anything other than nonsense to an casual onlooker. Or maybe that's not true. In any case, sing them out anyway; not because they're important or profitable, but simply because they're in you. I think the weirdest, silliest impulses that lurk within are probably closer to our real selves than the personas we develop to navigate most social interactions anyway.

But have you ever been silly with someone? Like really silly? My cousin Rocco and I used to have lengthy conversations in complete gibberish. It was mostly disgusting grunts and fart sounds (and a lot of Jabba the Hutt), but it's probably the closest we've ever been.

It may be an odd soapbox to stand on, but I think being silly is important.

Haunted Safari is pencil sketched onto standard A4 paper (90 lb/146 GSM), inked with a Pentel pocket brush pen, as well as these impossible-to-find stationary store pens that I'm obsessed with (thank you to my friend Yoomee for consistently mailing them to me from South Korea). The comics are then scanned into a computer and colored digitally. I couldn't tell you this is the most efficient way to make these, but it's my way.

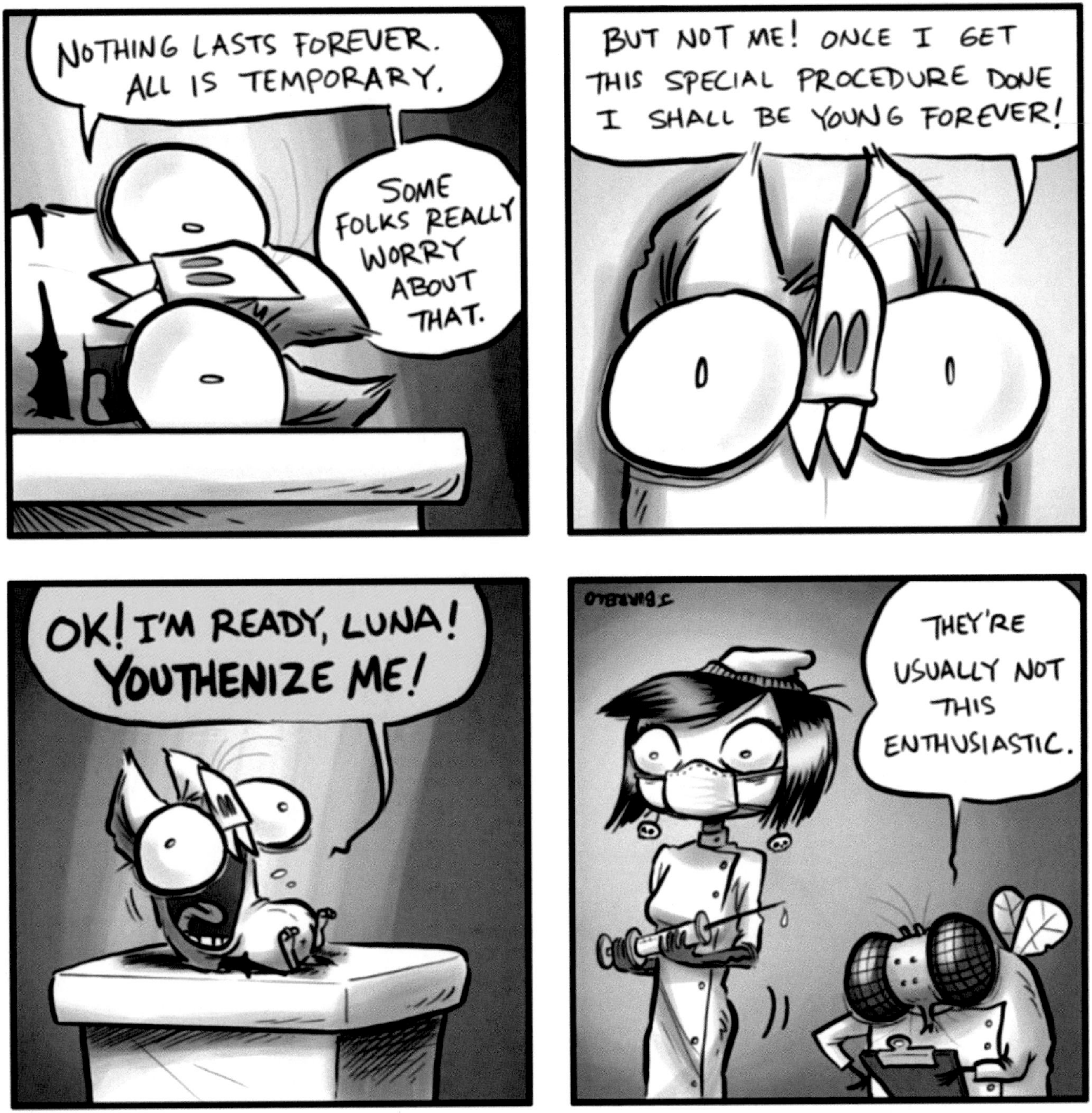
NOTHING LASTS FOREVER. ALL IS TEMPORARY.
SOME FOLKS REALLY WORRY ABOUT THAT.
BUT NOT ME! ONCE I GET THIS SPECIAL PROCEDURE DONE I SHALL BE YOUNG FOREVER!
OK! I'M READY, LUNA! YOUTHENIZE ME!
THEY'RE USUALLY NOT THIS ENTHUSIASTIC.

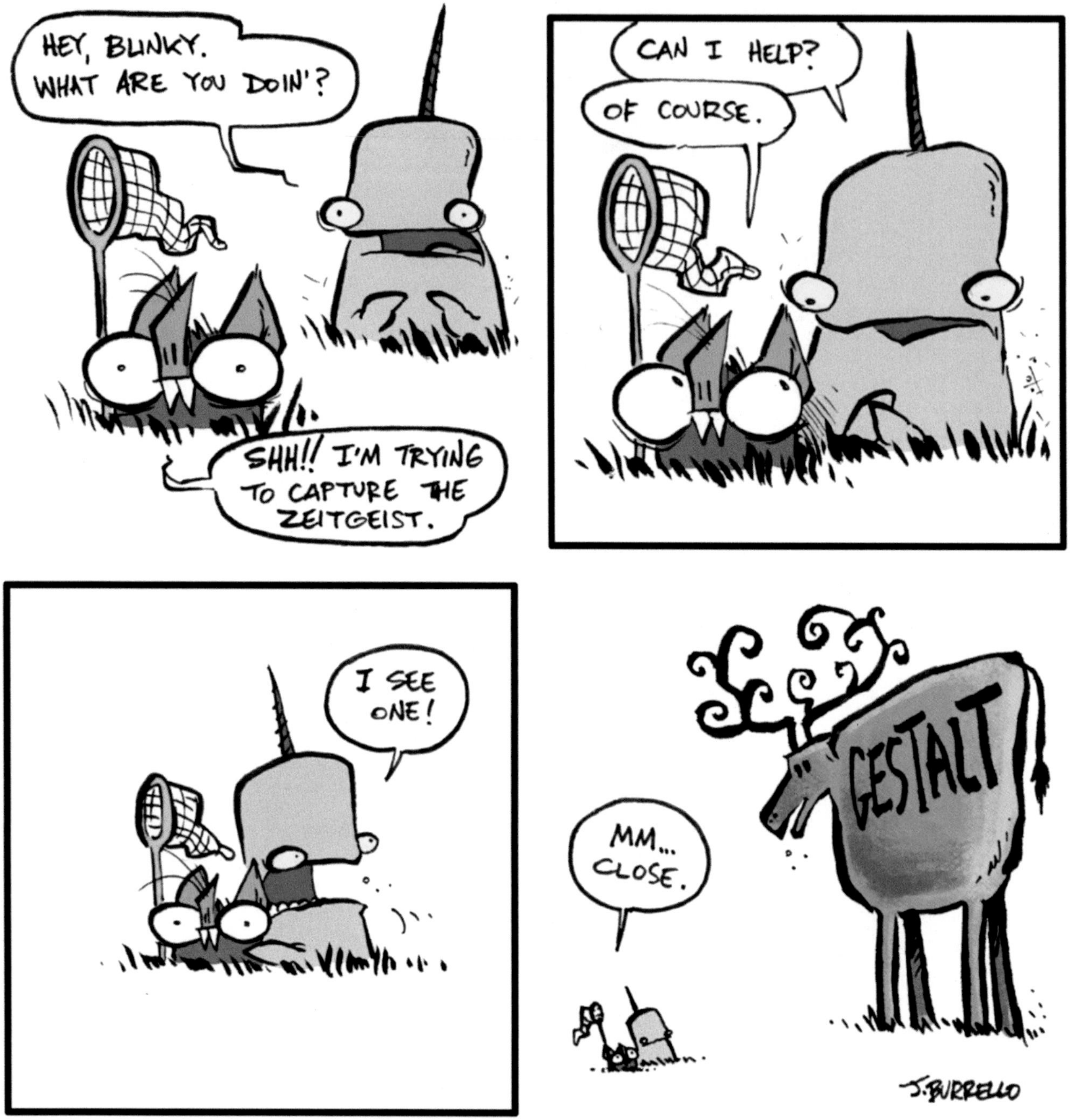
HEY, BLINKY. WHAT ARE YOU DOIN'?
SHH!! I'M TRYING TO CAPTURE THE ZEITGEIST.
CAN I HELP?
OF COURSE.
I SEE ONE!
MM... CLOSE.
GESTALT
J. BURRELLO

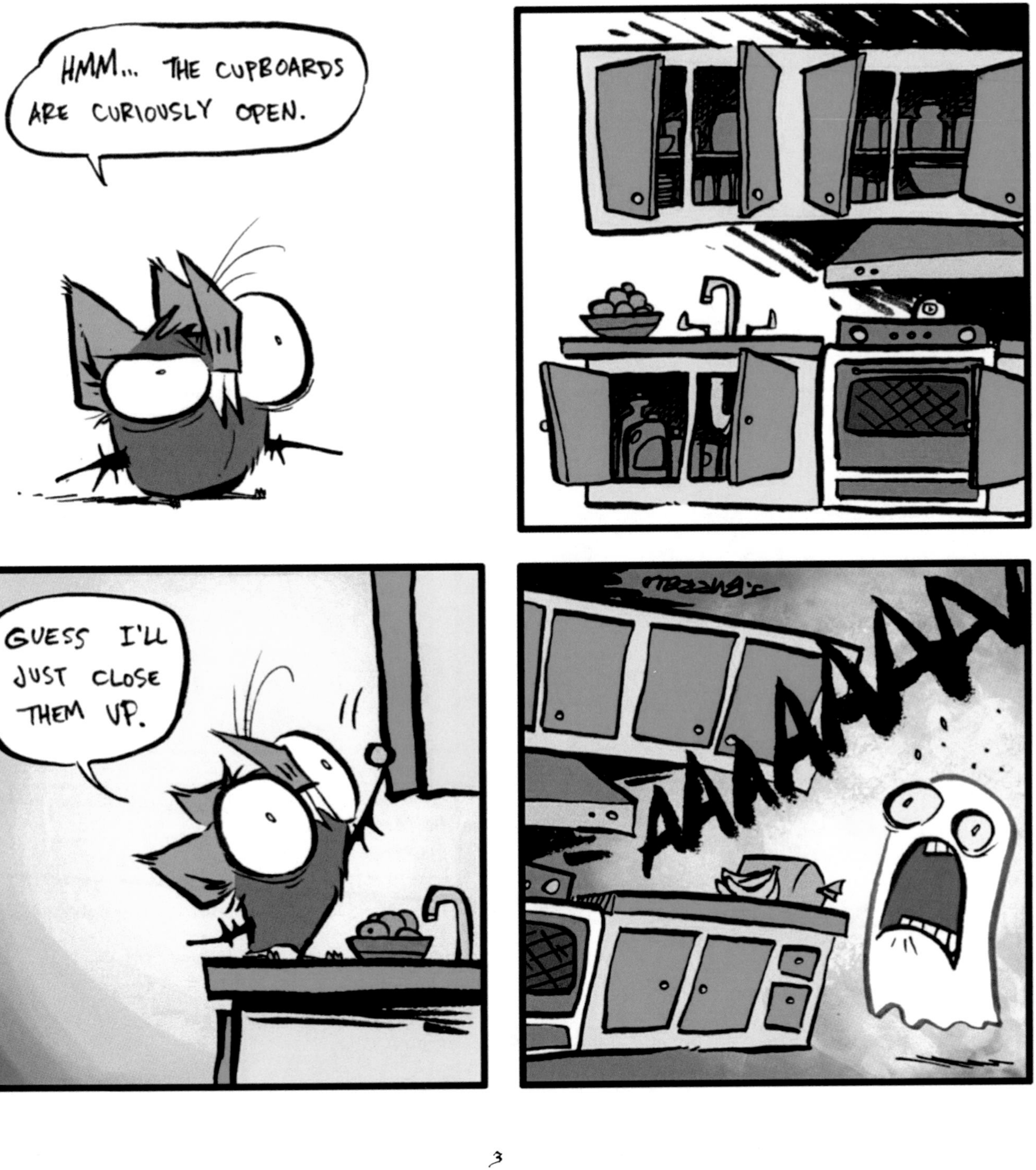
HMM... THE CUPBOARDS ARE CURIOUSLY OPEN.
GUESS I'LL JUST CLOSE THEM UP.

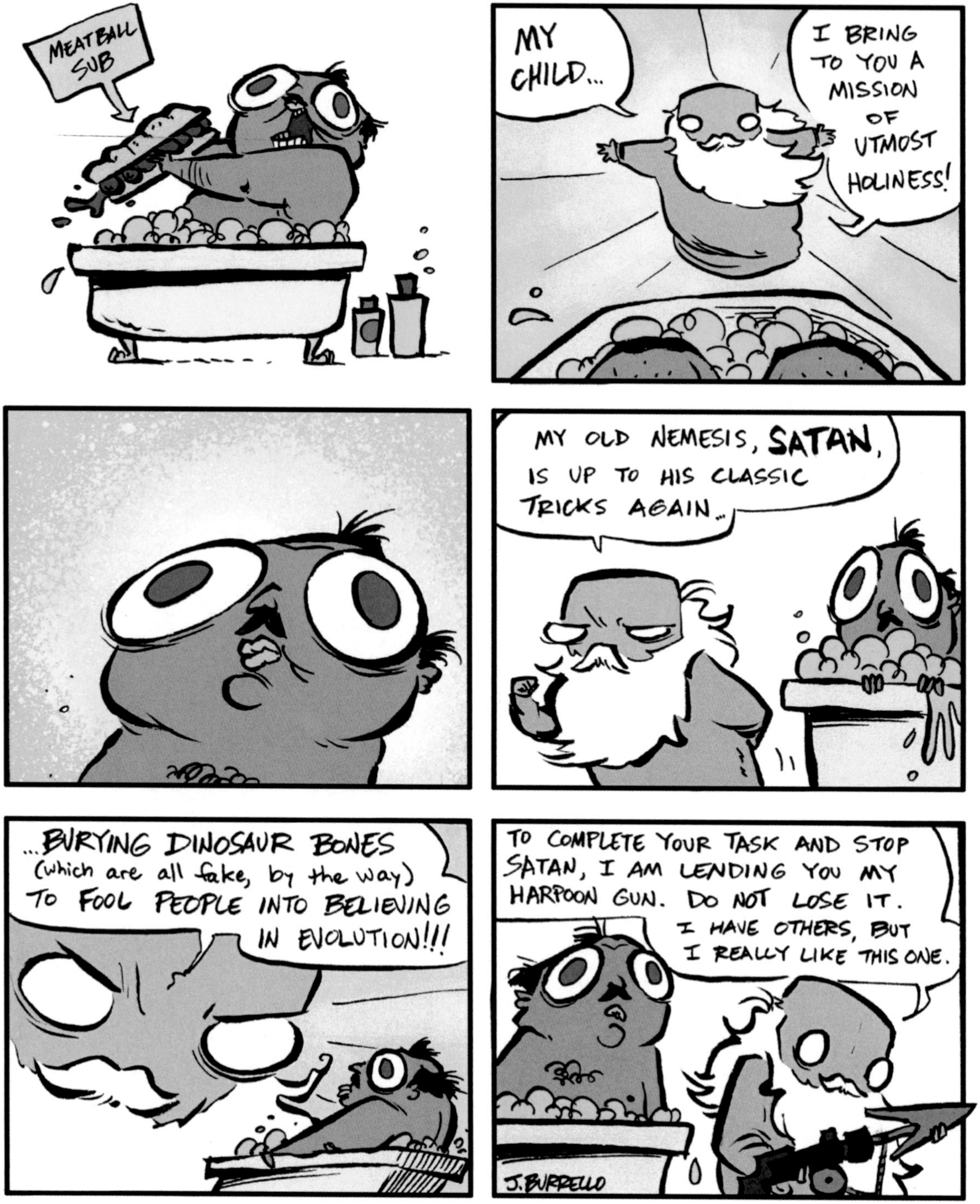
MEATBALL SUB
MY CHILD...
I BRING TO YOU A MISSION OF UTMOST HOLINESS!
MY OLD NEMESIS, SATAN, IS UP TO HIS CLASSIC TRICKS AGAIN...
...BURYING DINOSAUR BONES (which are all fake, by the way) TO FOOL PEOPLE INTO BELIEVING IN EVOLUTION!!!
TO COMPLETE YOUR TASK AND STOP SATAN, I AM LENDING YOU MY HARPOON GUN. DO NOT LOSE IT.
I HAVE OTHERS, BUT I REALLY LIKE THIS ONE.
J.BURRELLO

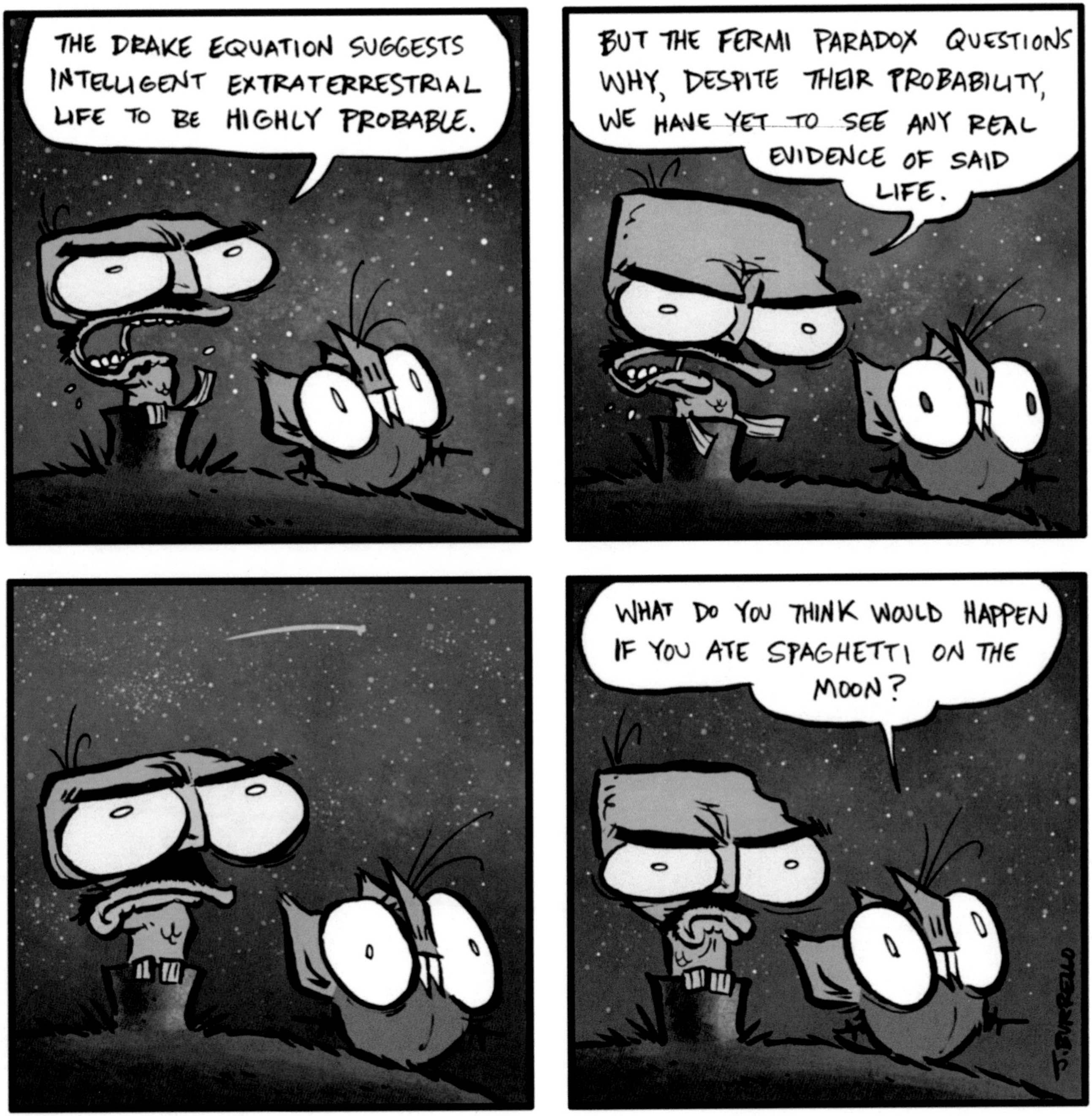
THE DRAKE EQUATION SUGGESTS INTELLIGENT EXTRATERRESTRIAL LIFE TO BE HIGHLY PROBABLE.
BUT THE FERMI PARADOX QUESTIONS WHY, DESPITE THEIR PROBABILITY, WE HAVE YET TO SEE ANY REAL EVIDENCE OF SAID LIFE.
WHAT DO YOU THINK WOULD HAPPEN IF YOU ATE SPAGHETTI ON THE MOON?
J. BURRELLO

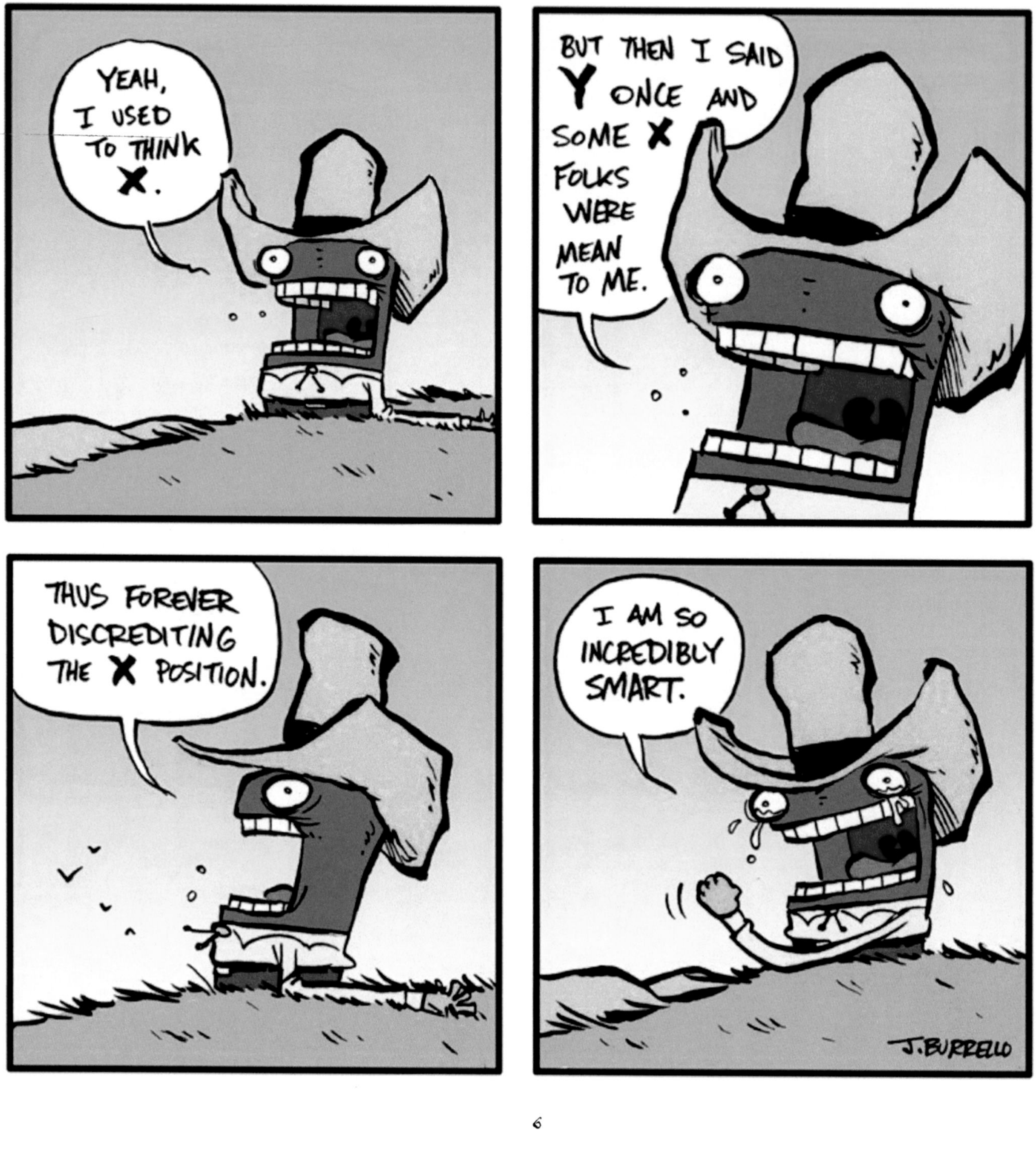
YEAH, I USED TO THINK X.
BUT THEN I SAID Y ONCE AND SOME X FOLKS WERE MEAN TO ME.
THUS FOREVER DISCREDITING THE X POSITION.
I AM SO INCREDIBLY SMART.
J.BURRELLO

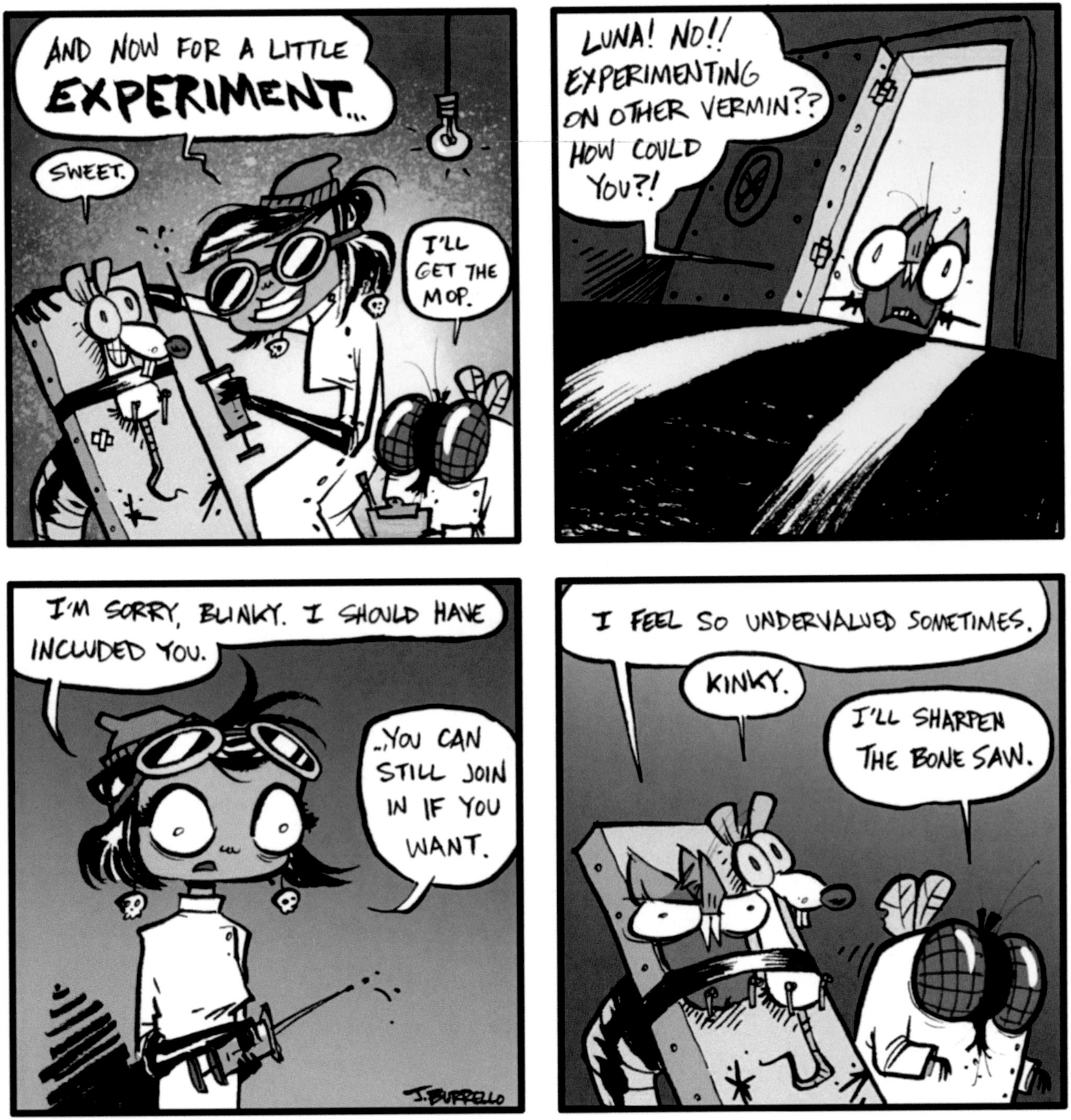
AND NOW FOR A LITTLE EXPERIMENT...
SWEET.
I'LL GET THE MOP.
LUNA! NO!! EXPERIMENTING ON OTHER VERMIN?? HOW COULD YOU?!
I'M SORRY, BLINKY. I SHOULD HAVE INCLUDED YOU.
..YOU CAN STILL JOIN IN IF YOU WANT.
J. BURRELLO
I FEEL SO UNDERVALUED SOMETIMES.
KINKY.
I'LL SHARPEN THE BONE SAW.

BLINKY

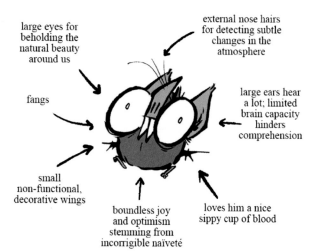

large eyes for beholding the natural beauty around us

external nose hairs for detecting subtle changes in the atmosphere

fangs

large ears hear a lot; limited brain capacity hinders comprehension

small non-functional, decorative wings

boundless joy and optimism stemming from incorrigible naïveté

loves him a nice sippy cup of blood

SAL

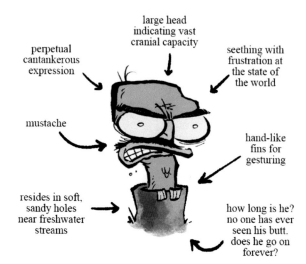

large head indicating vast cranial capacity

perpetual cantankerous expression

seething with frustration at the state of the world

mustache

hand-like fins for gesturing

resides in soft, sandy holes near freshwater streams

how long is he? no one has ever seen his butt. does he go on forever?

SPATSBY

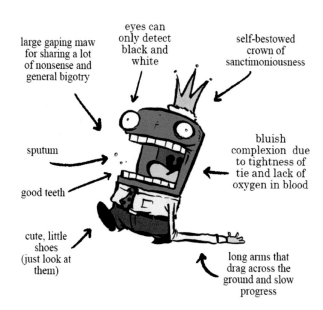

large gaping maw for sharing a lot of nonsense and general bigotry

eyes can only detect black and white

self-bestowed crown of sanctimoniousness

sputum

bluish complexion due to tightness of tie and lack of oxygen in blood

good teeth

cute, little shoes (just look at them)

long arms that drag across the ground and slow progress

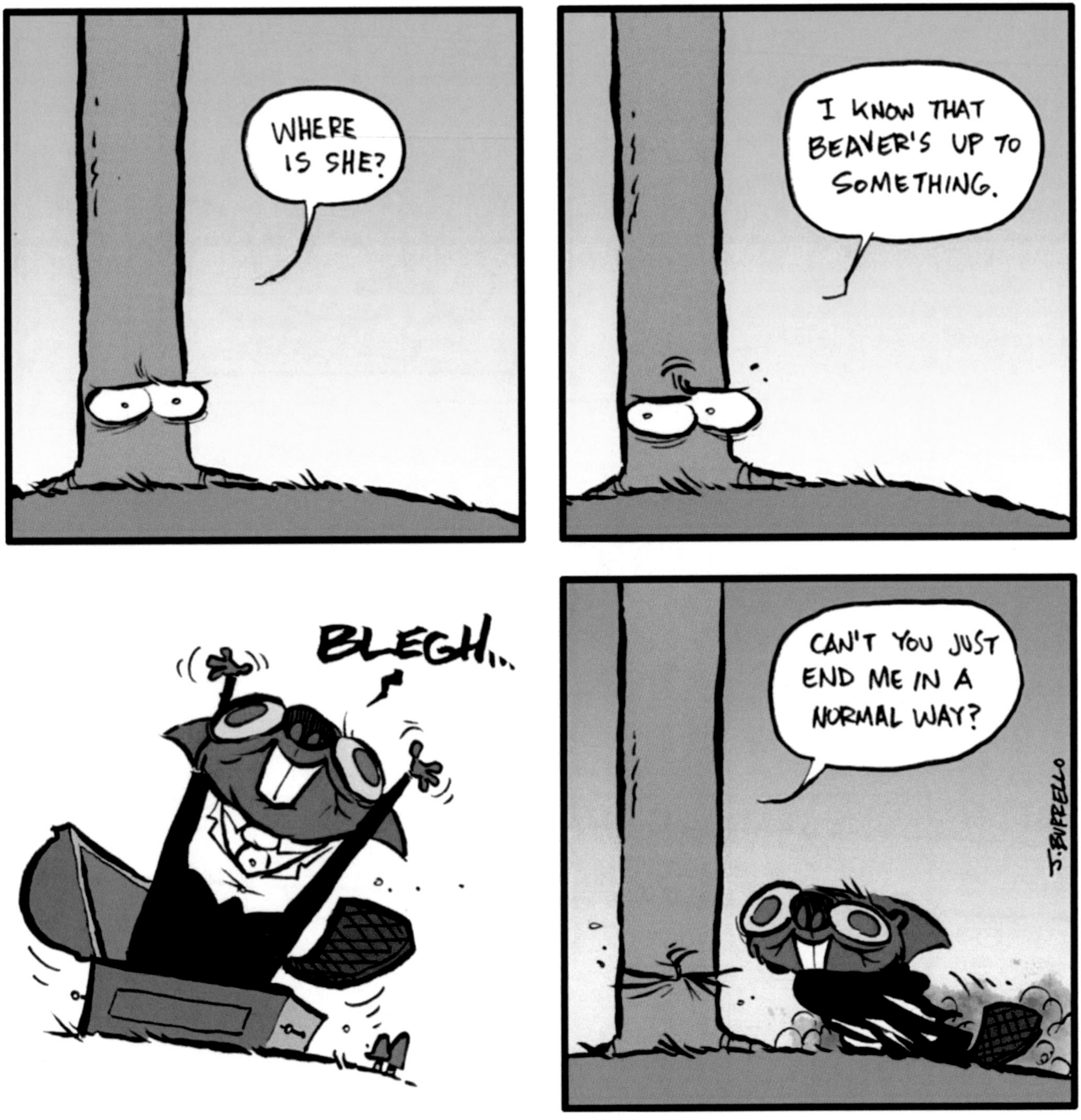
WHERE IS SHE?
I KNOW THAT BEAVER'S UP TO SOMETHING.
BLEGH...
CAN'T YOU JUST END ME IN A NORMAL WAY?
J. BURRELLO

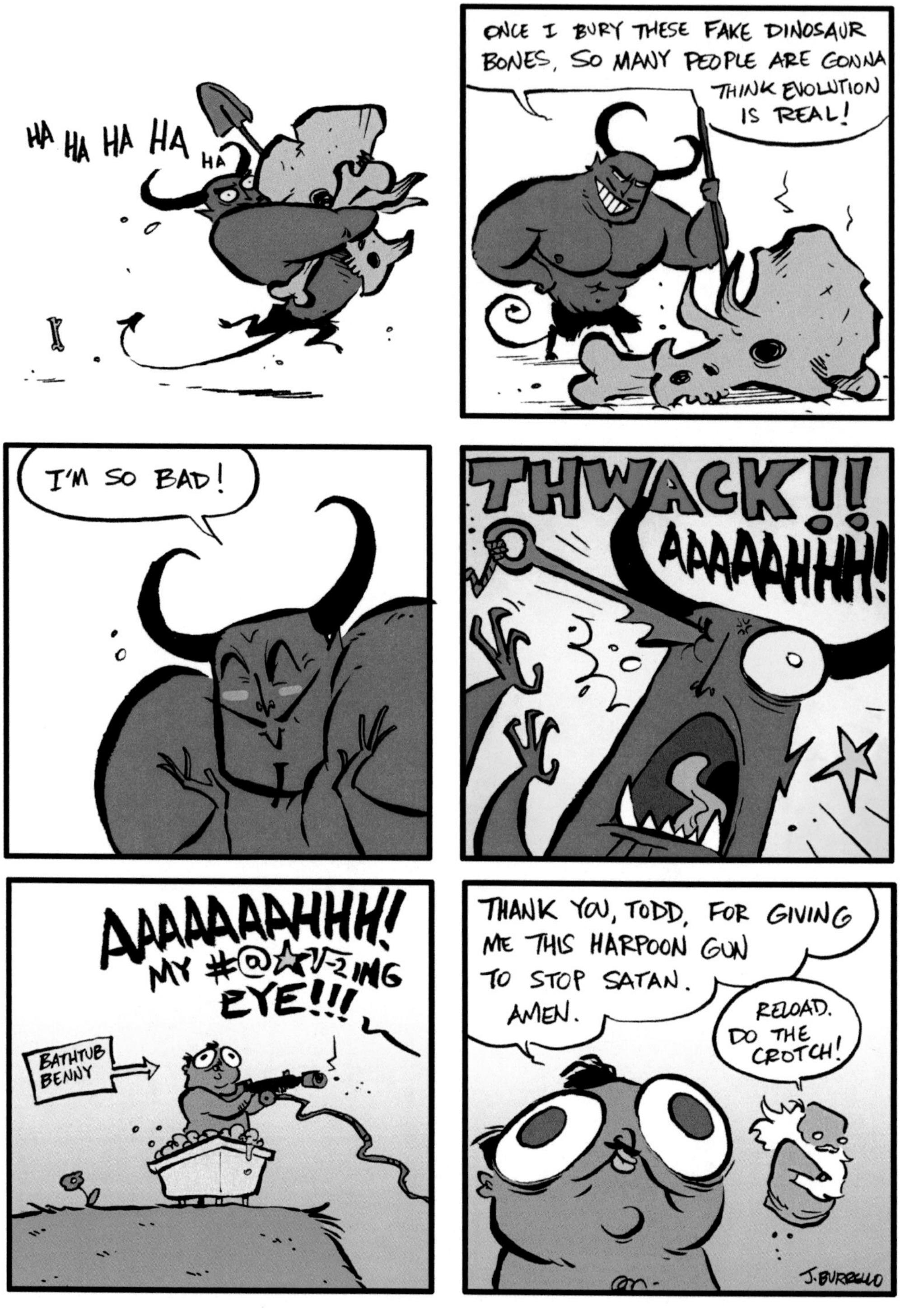
HA HA HA HA HA
ONCE I BURY THESE FAKE DINOSAUR BONES, SO MANY PEOPLE ARE GONNA THINK EVOLUTION IS REAL!
I'M SO BAD!
THWACK!!
AAAAAHHH!
AAAAAAHHH! MY #@☆√-2ING EYE!!!
BATHTUB BENNY
THANK YOU, TODD, FOR GIVING ME THIS HARPOON GUN TO STOP SATAN. AMEN.
RELOAD. DO THE CROTCH!
J. BURRELLO

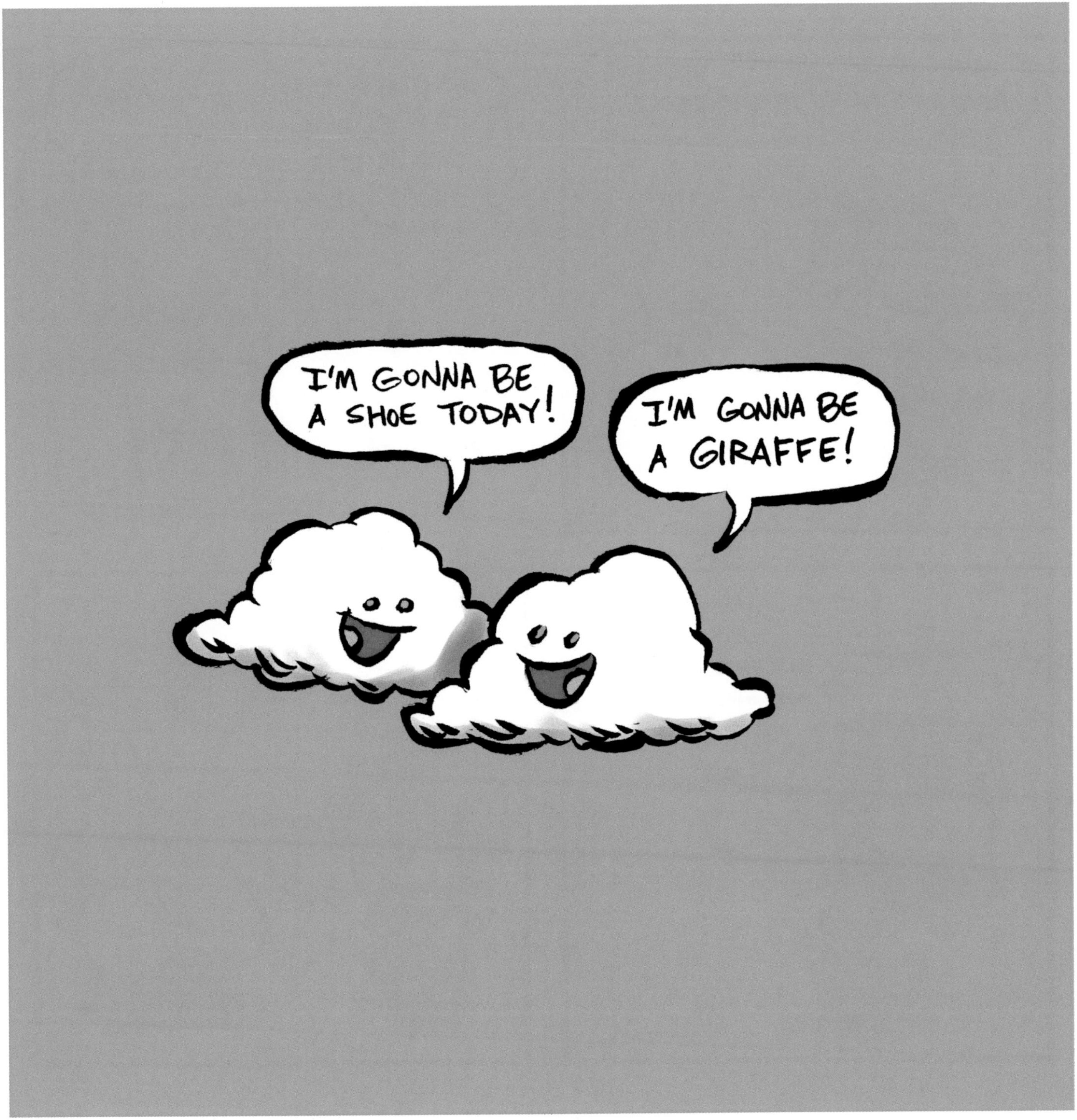
I'M GONNA BE A SHOE TODAY!
I'M GONNA BE A GIRAFFE!

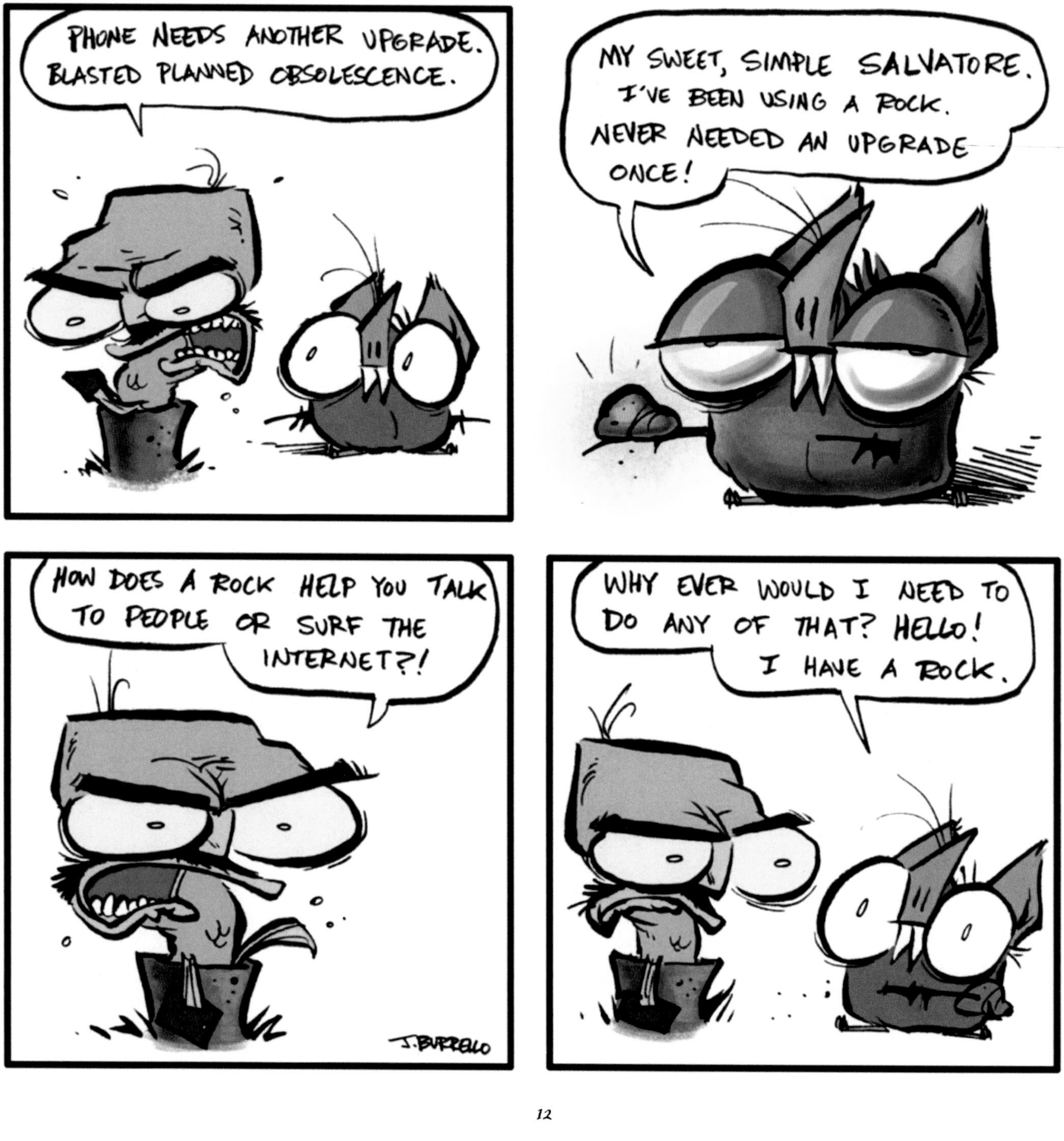
PHONE NEEDS ANOTHER UPGRADE. BLASTED PLANNED OBSOLESCENCE.
MY SWEET, SIMPLE SALVATORE. I'VE BEEN USING A ROCK. NEVER NEEDED AN UPGRADE ONCE!
HOW DOES A ROCK HELP YOU TALK TO PEOPLE OR SURF THE INTERNET?!
WHY EVER WOULD I NEED TO DO ANY OF THAT? HELLO! I HAVE A ROCK.
J. BURRELLO

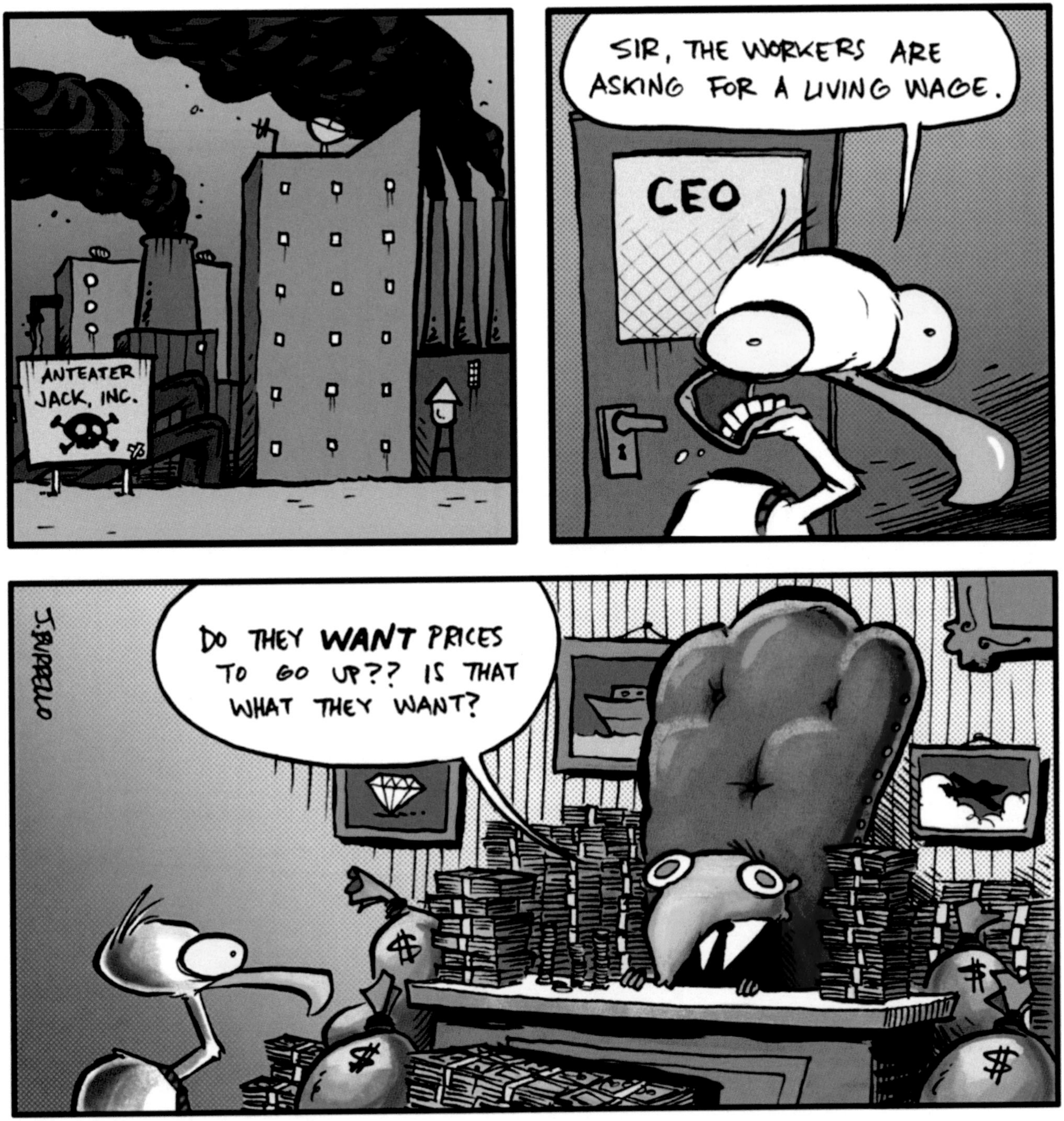
ANTEATER
JACK, INC.
SIR, THE WORKERS ARE ASKING FOR A LIVING WAGE.
CEO
DO THEY **WANT** PRICES TO GO UP?? IS THAT WHAT THEY WANT?

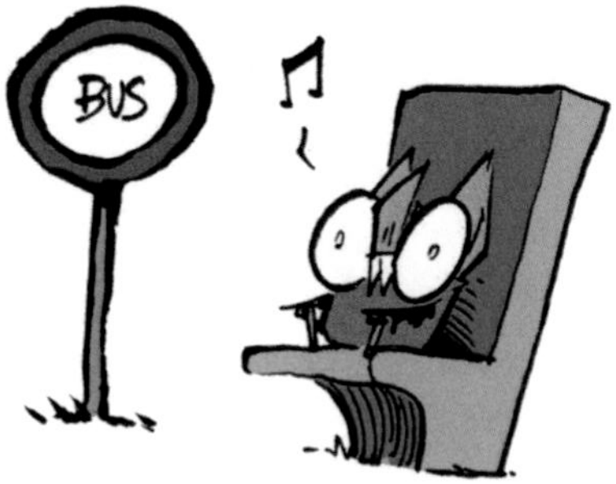
BUS

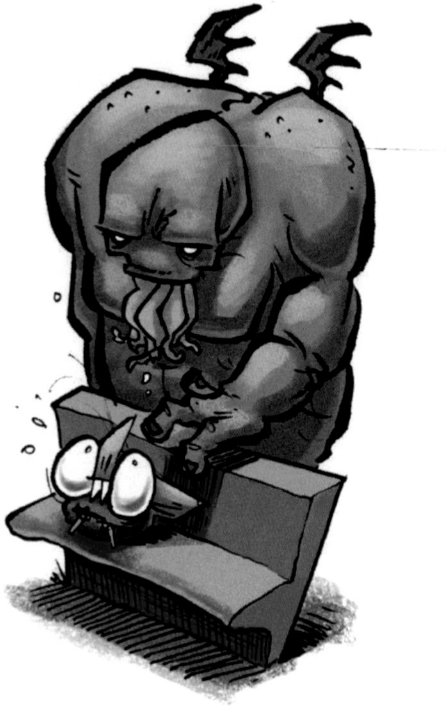

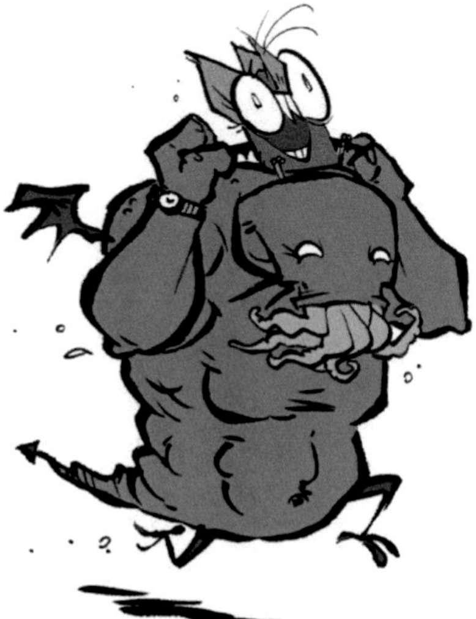

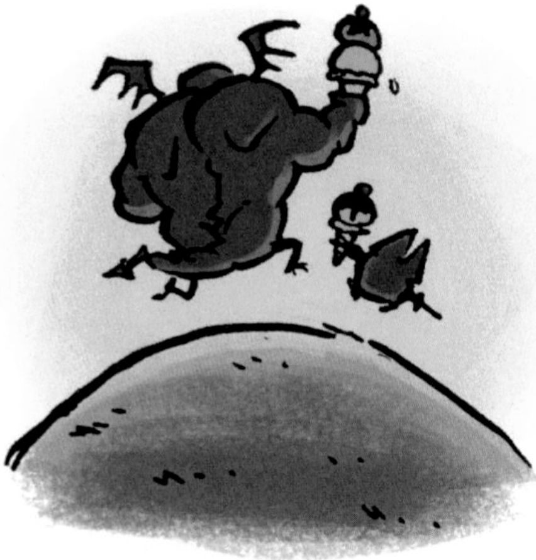

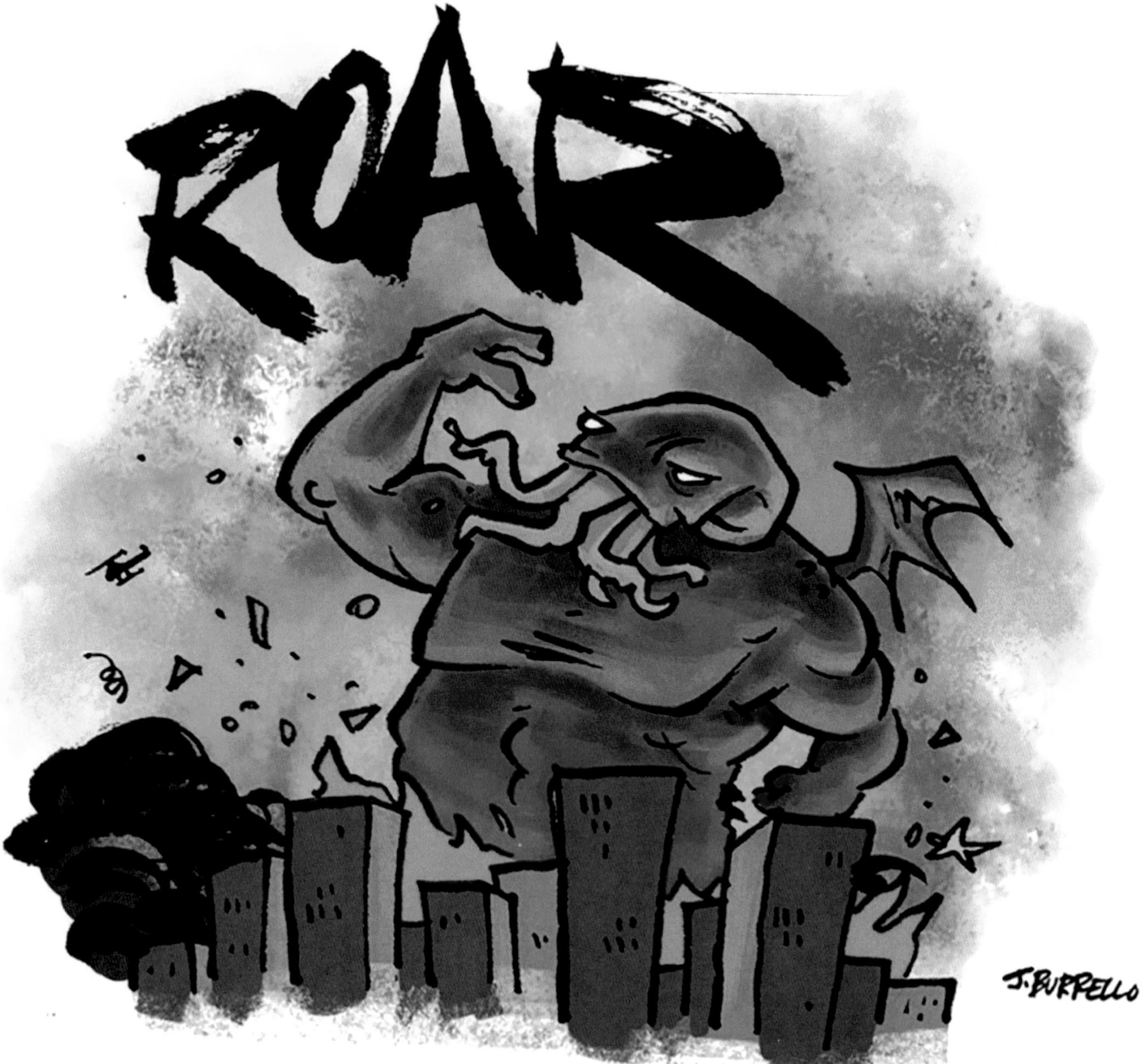
ROAR
J. BURRELLO

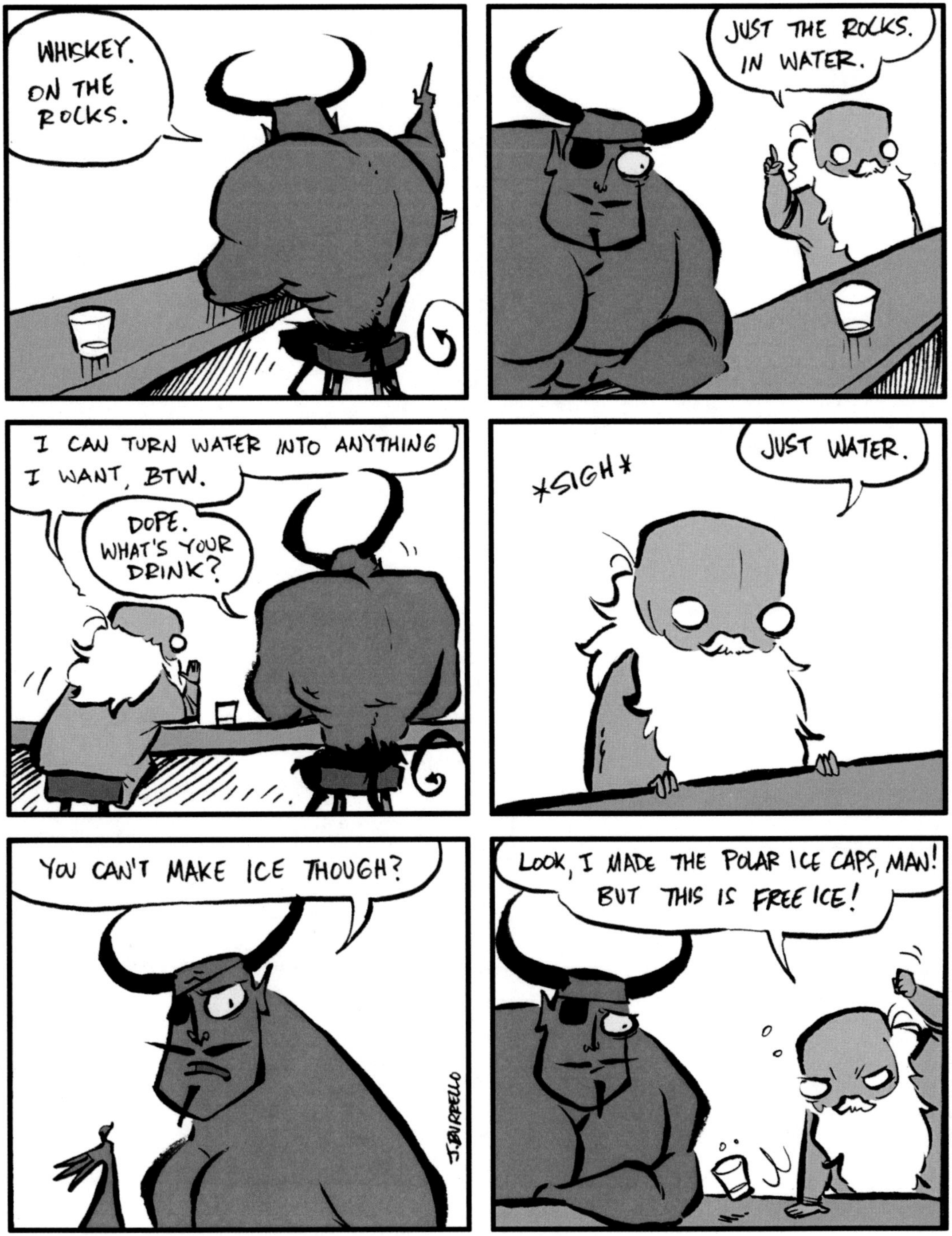
WHISKEY. ON THE ROCKS.
JUST THE ROCKS. IN WATER.
I CAN TURN WATER INTO ANYTHING I WANT, BTW.
DOPE. WHAT'S YOUR DRINK?
SIGH
JUST WATER.
YOU CAN'T MAKE ICE THOUGH?
J. BURRELLO
LOOK, I MADE THE POLAR ICE CAPS, MAN! BUT THIS IS FREE ICE!

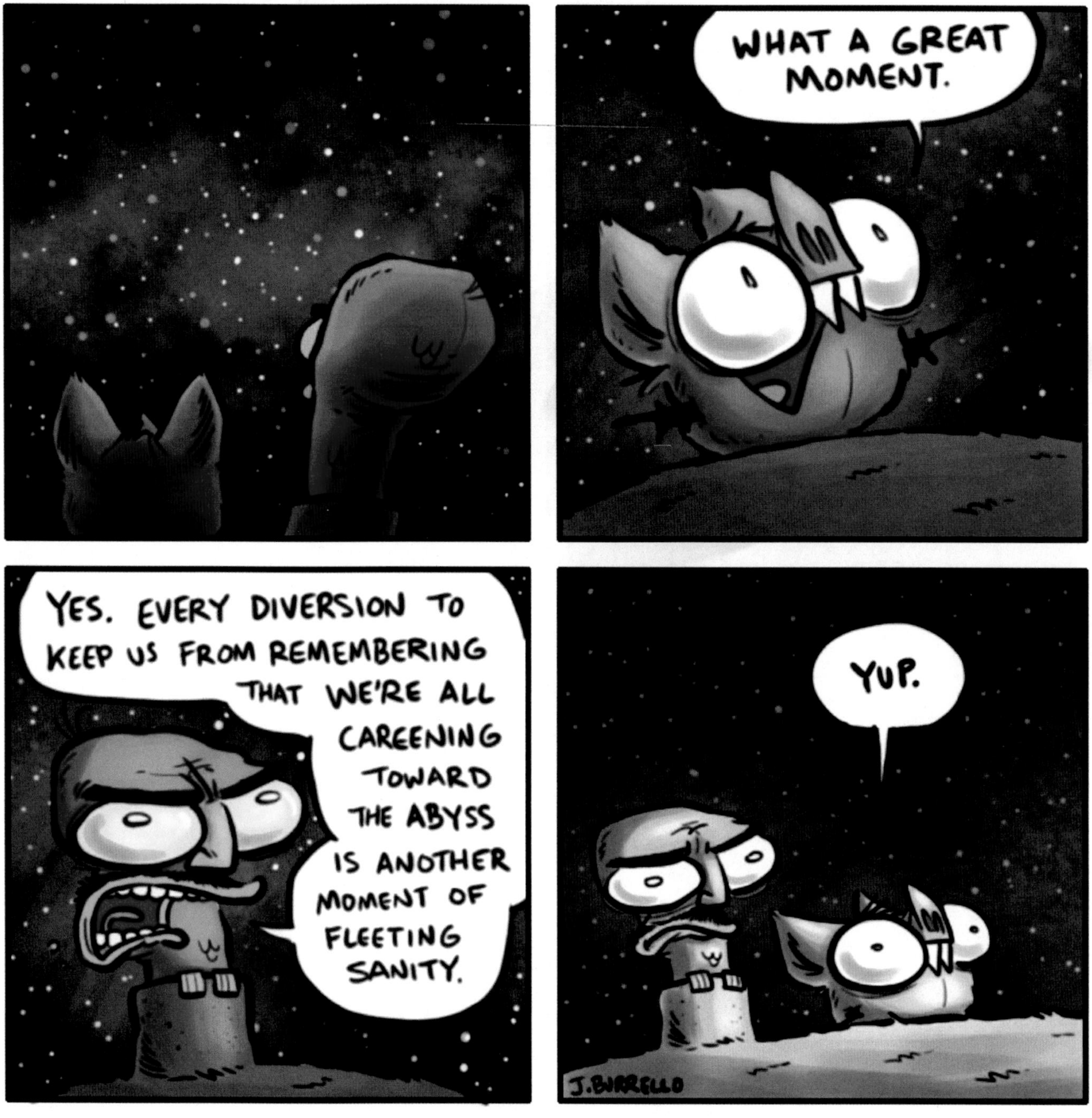
WHAT A GREAT MOMENT.
YES. EVERY DIVERSION TO KEEP US FROM REMEMBERING THAT WE'RE ALL CAREENING TOWARD THE ABYSS IS ANOTHER MOMENT OF FLEETING SANITY.
YUP.
J.BURRELLO

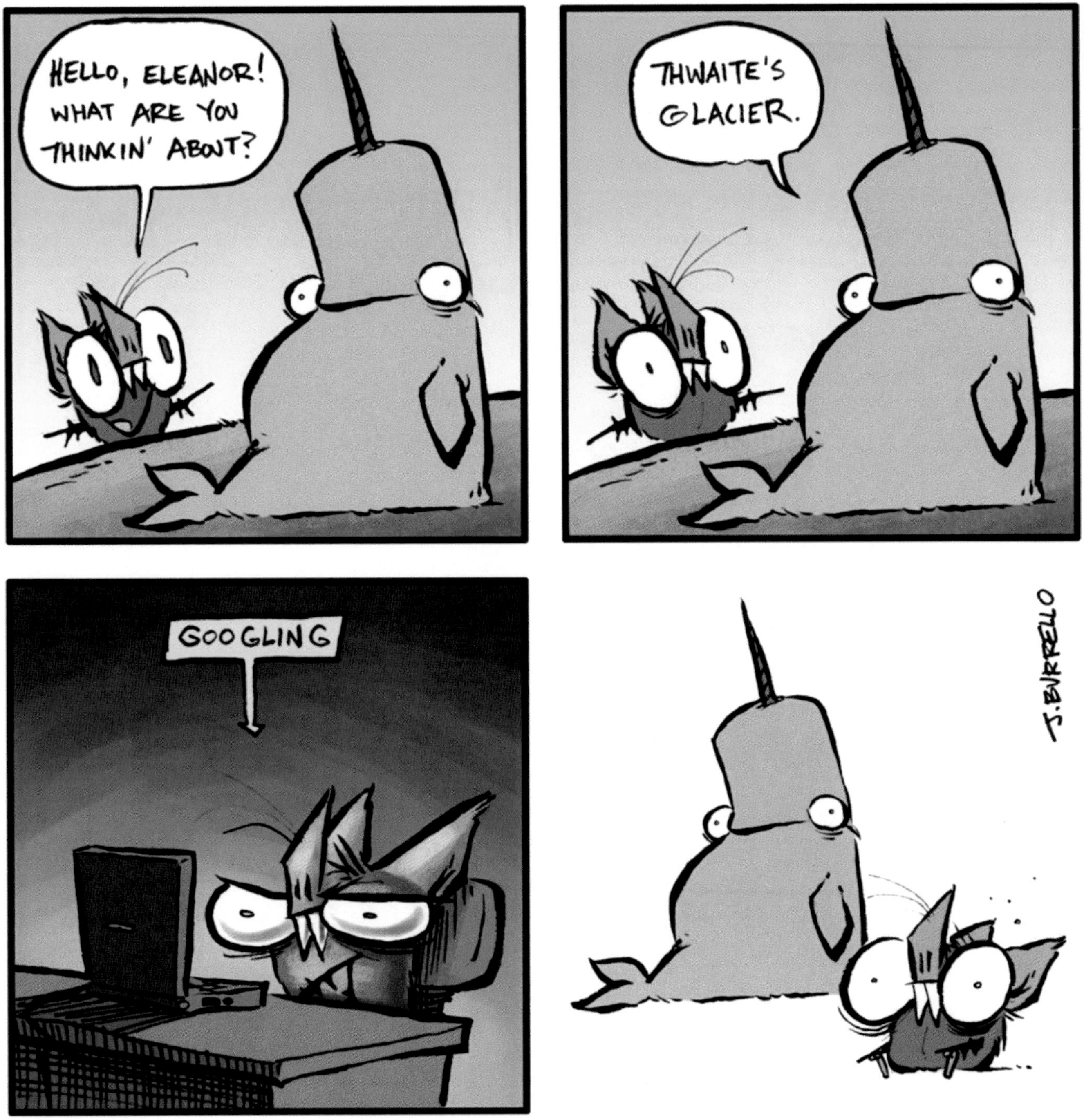
HELLO, ELEANOR! WHAT ARE YOU THINKIN' ABOUT?
THWAITE'S GLACIER.
GOOGLING
J. BURRELLO

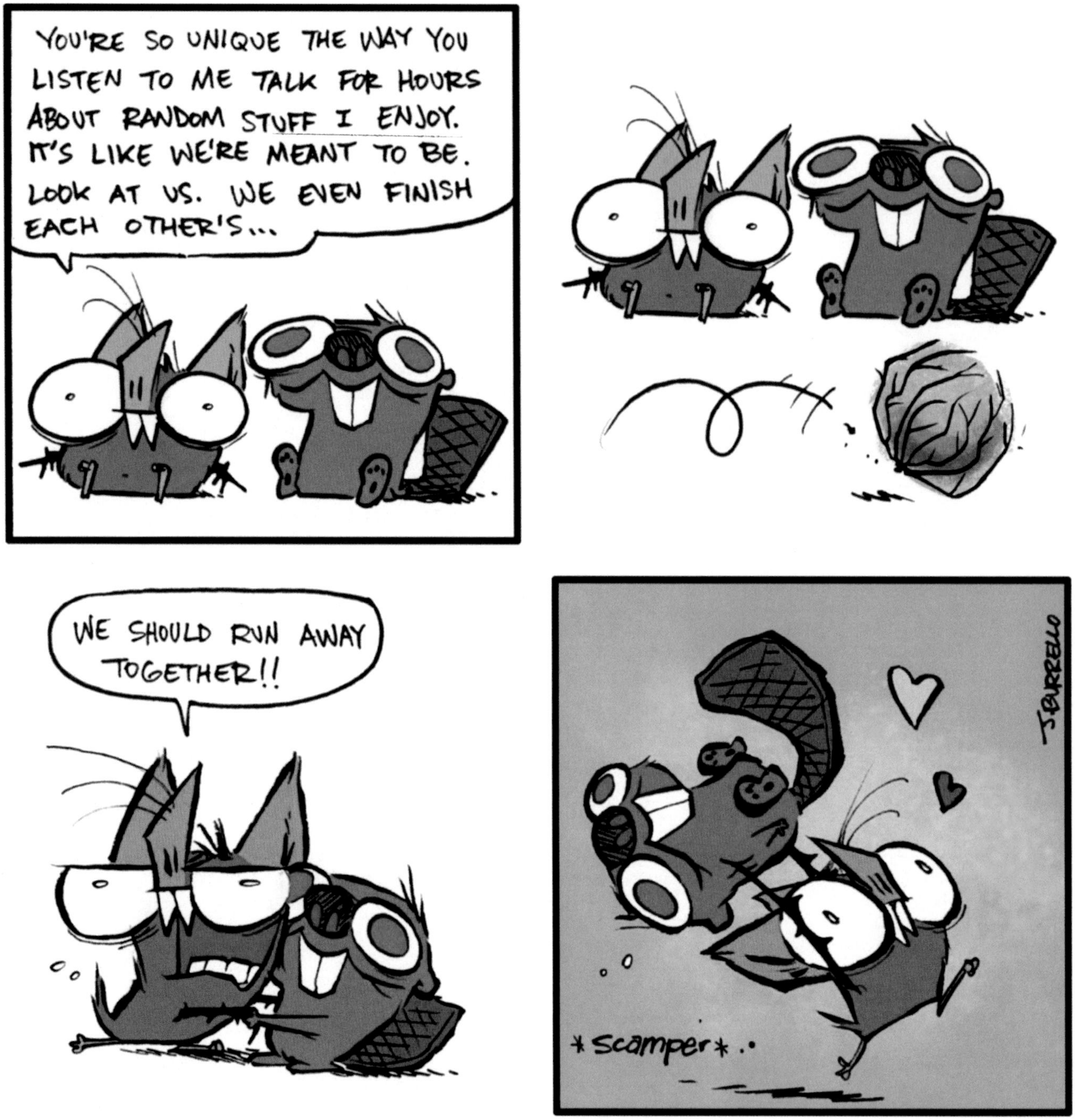
YOU'RE SO UNIQUE THE WAY YOU LISTEN TO ME TALK FOR HOURS ABOUT RANDOM STUFF I ENJOY. IT'S LIKE WE'RE MEANT TO BE. LOOK AT US. WE EVEN FINISH EACH OTHER'S...
WE SHOULD RUN AWAY TOGETHER!!
J.BURRELLO
scamper

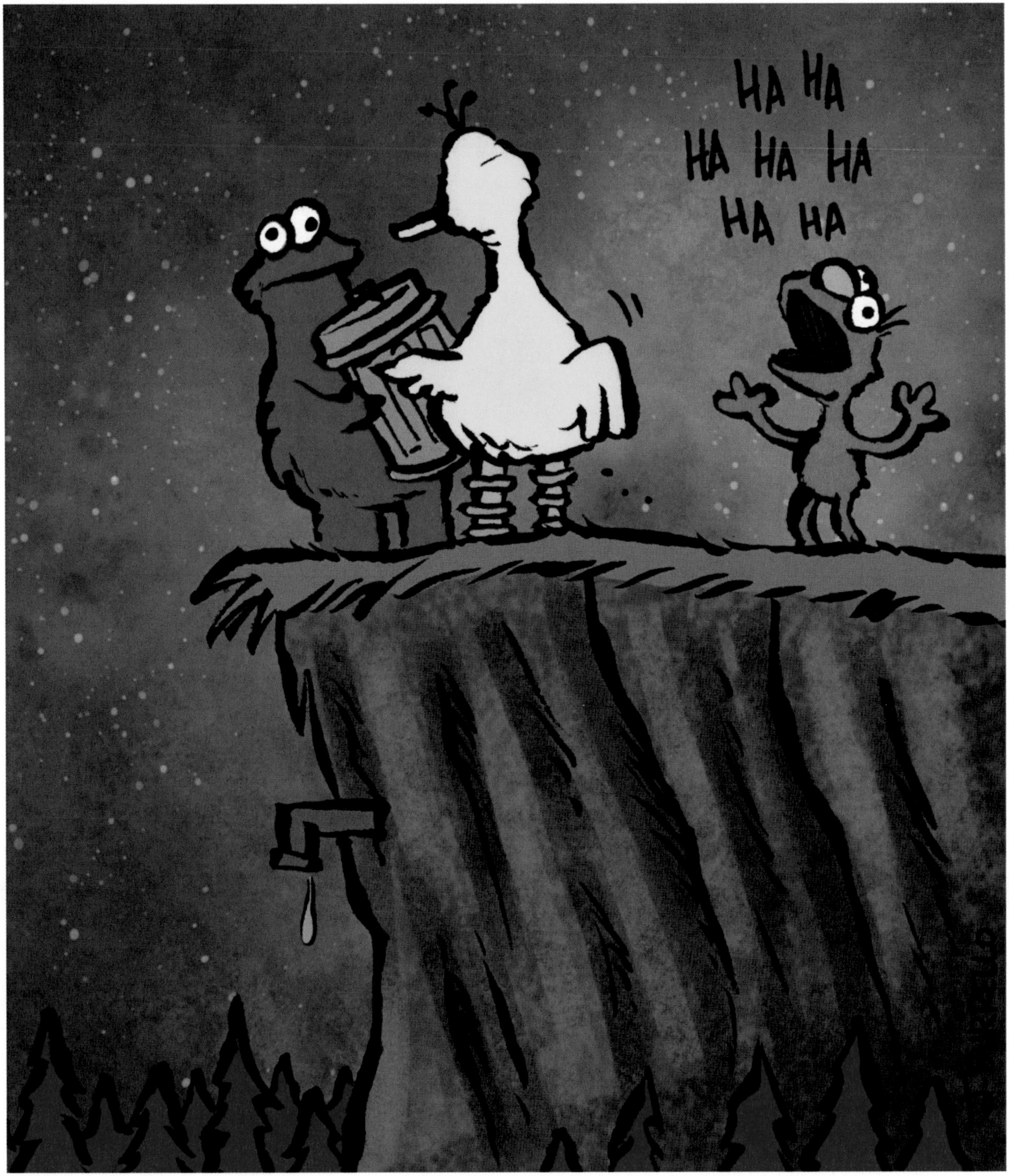
HA HA
HA HA HA
HA HA

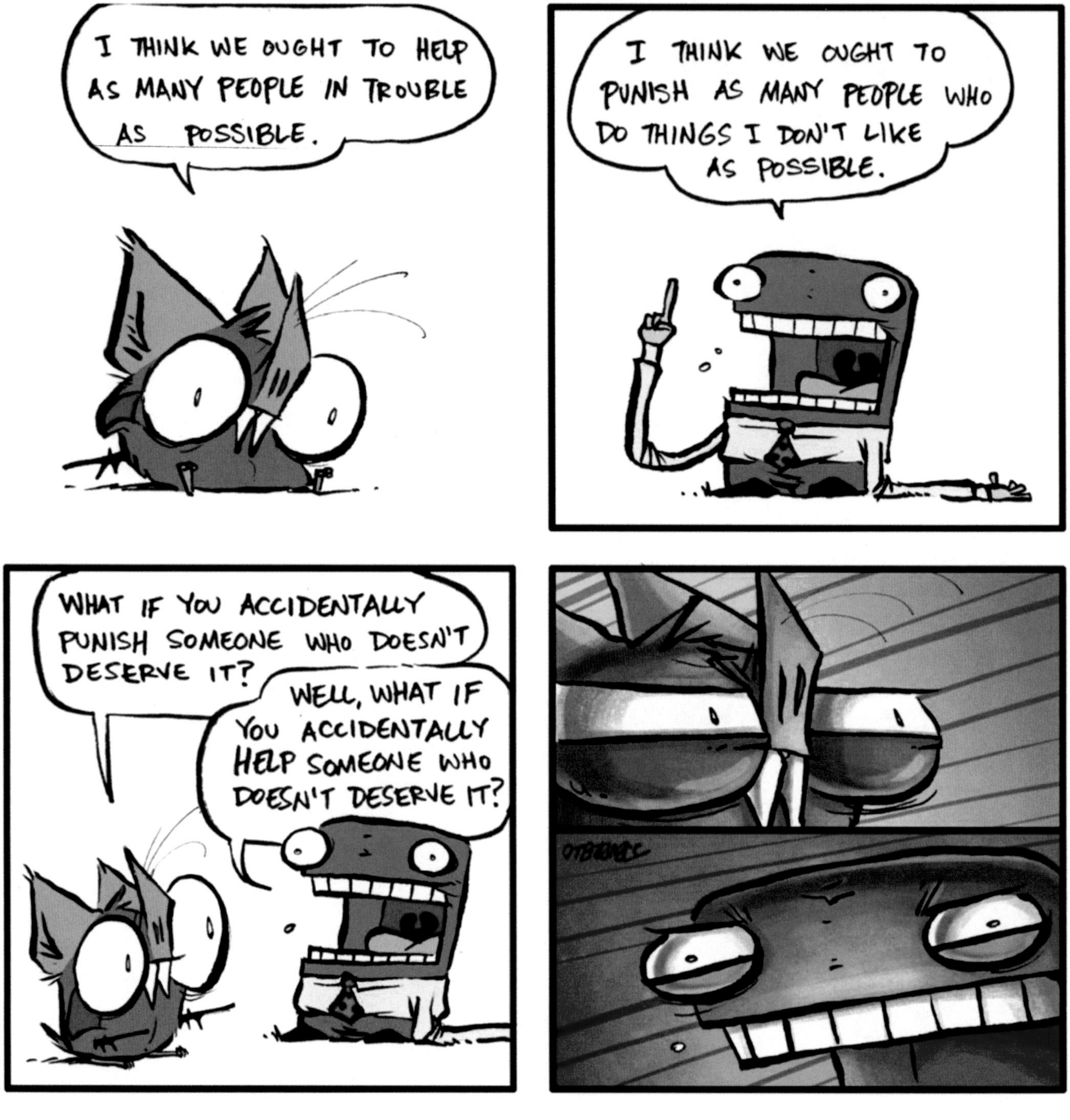
I THINK WE OUGHT TO HELP AS MANY PEOPLE IN TROUBLE AS POSSIBLE.
I THINK WE OUGHT TO PUNISH AS MANY PEOPLE WHO DO THINGS I DON'T LIKE AS POSSIBLE.
WHAT IF YOU ACCIDENTALLY PUNISH SOMEONE WHO DOESN'T DESERVE IT?
WELL, WHAT IF YOU ACCIDENTALLY HELP SOMEONE WHO DOESN'T DESERVE IT?

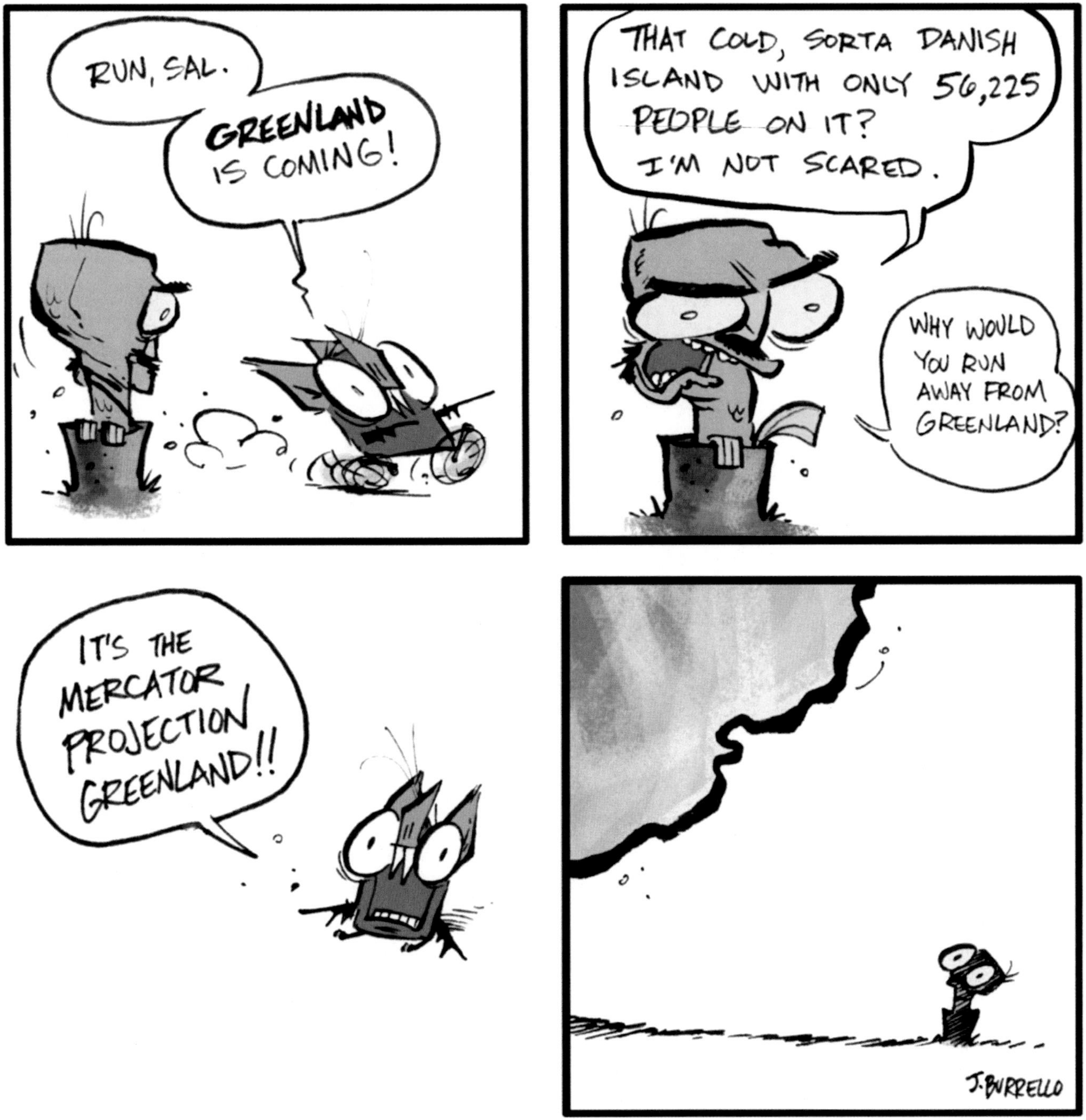
RUN, SAL.
GREENLAND IS COMING!
THAT COLD, SORTA DANISH ISLAND WITH ONLY 56,225 PEOPLE ON IT? I'M NOT SCARED.
WHY WOULD YOU RUN AWAY FROM GREENLAND?
IT'S THE MERCATOR PROJECTION GREENLAND!!
J. BURRELLO

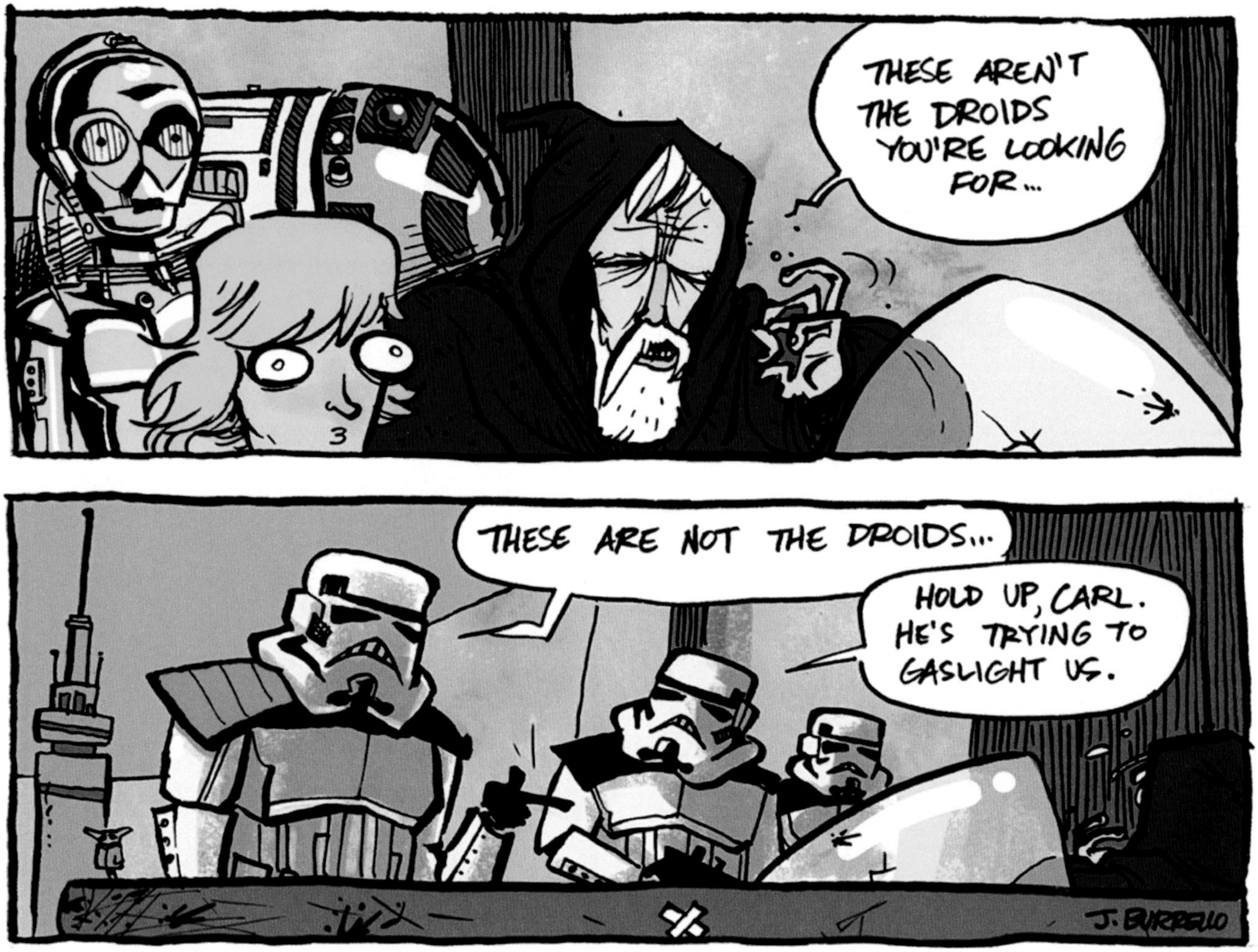
THESE AREN'T THE DROIDS YOU'RE LOOKING FOR...
THESE ARE NOT THE DROIDS...
HOLD UP, CARL. HE'S TRYING TO GASLIGHT US.
J. BURRELLO

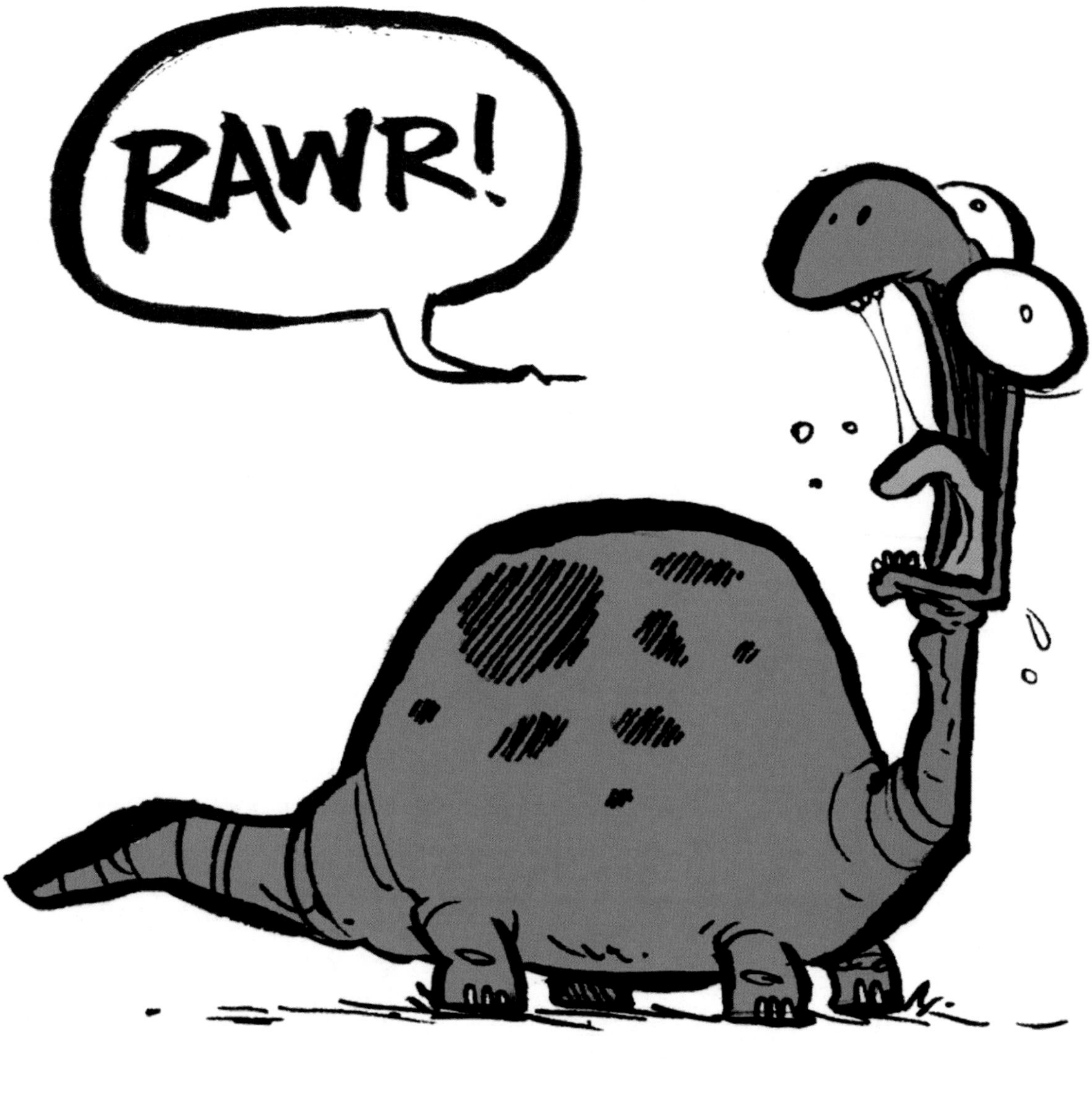
RAWR!

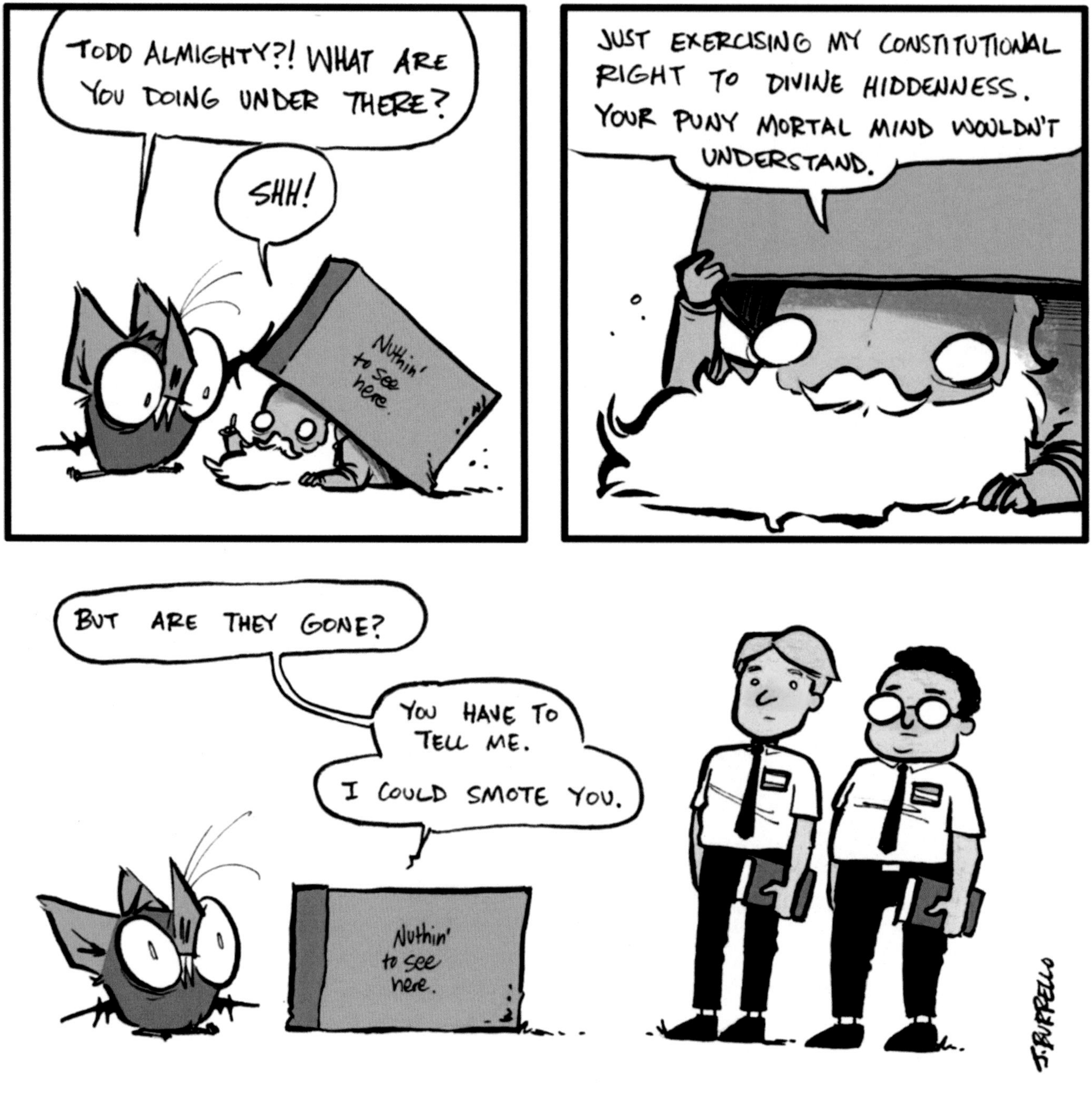
TODD ALMIGHTY?! WHAT ARE YOU DOING UNDER THERE?
SHH!
Nuthin' to see here.
JUST EXERCISING MY CONSTITUTIONAL RIGHT TO DIVINE HIDDENNESS. YOUR PUNY MORTAL MIND WOULDN'T UNDERSTAND.
BUT ARE THEY GONE?
YOU HAVE TO TELL ME.
I COULD SMOTE YOU.
Nuthin' to see here.
J. BURRELLO

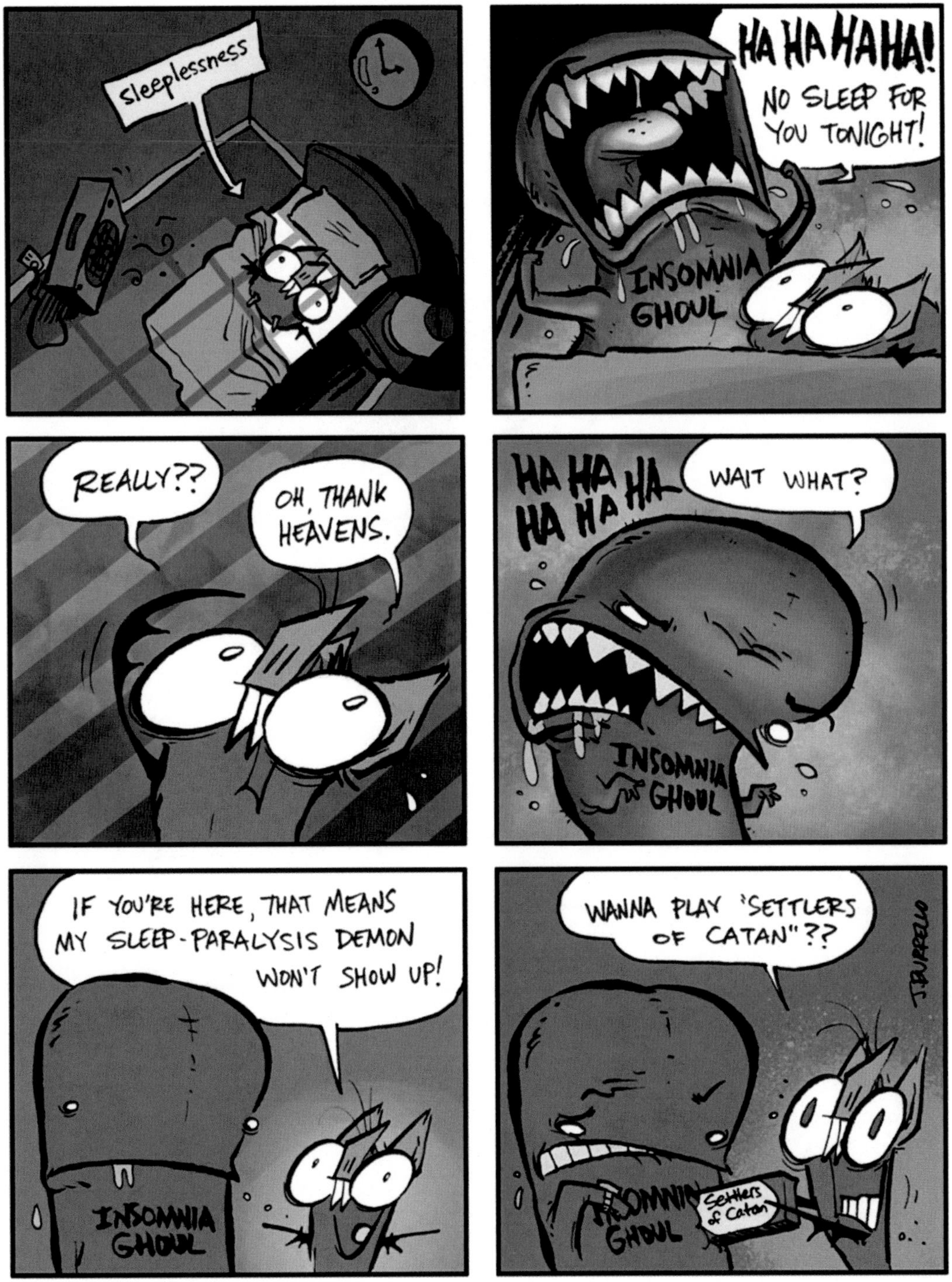
sleeplessness
HA HA HA HA!
NO SLEEP FOR YOU TONIGHT!
INSOMNIA GHOUL
REALLY??
OH, THANK HEAVENS.
HA HA HA HA HA HA
WAIT WHAT?
INSOMNIA GHOUL
IF YOU'RE HERE, THAT MEANS MY SLEEP-PARALYSIS DEMON WON'T SHOW UP!
INSOMNIA GHOUL
WANNA PLAY "SETTLERS OF CATAN"??
Settlers of Catan
J.BURRELLO

BEAVER

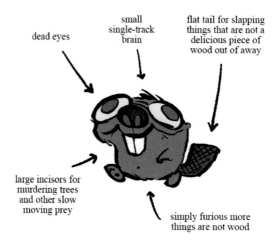

dead eyes

small single-track brain

flat tail for slapping things that are not a delicious piece of wood out of away

large incisors for murdering trees and other slow moving prey

simply furious more things are not wood

ELEANOR

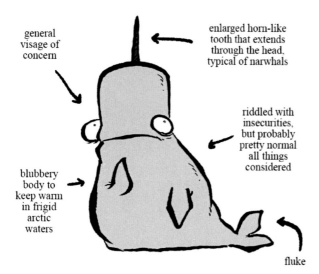

general visage of concern

enlarged horn-like tooth that extends through the head, typical of narwhals

riddled with insecurities, but probably pretty normal all things considered

blubbery body to keep warm in frigid arctic waters

fluke

OTTER

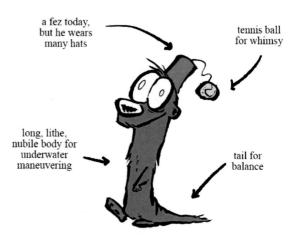

a fez today, but he wears many hats

tennis ball for whimsy

long, lithe, nubile body for underwater maneuvering

tail for balance

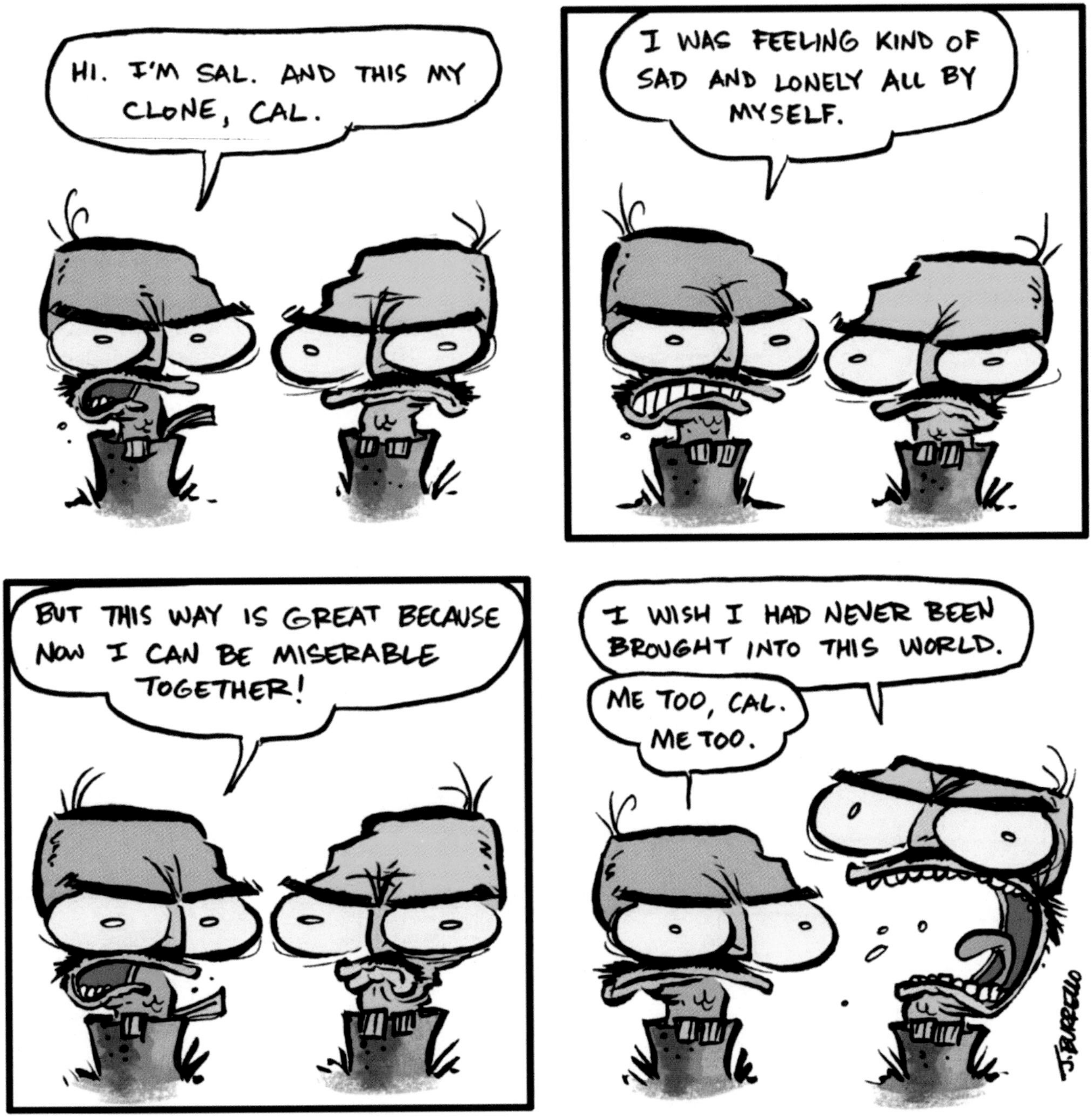
HI. I'M SAL. AND THIS MY CLONE, CAL.
I WAS FEELING KIND OF SAD AND LONELY ALL BY MYSELF.
BUT THIS WAY IS GREAT BECAUSE NOW I CAN BE MISERABLE TOGETHER!
I WISH I HAD NEVER BEEN BROUGHT INTO THIS WORLD.
ME TOO, CAL. ME TOO.

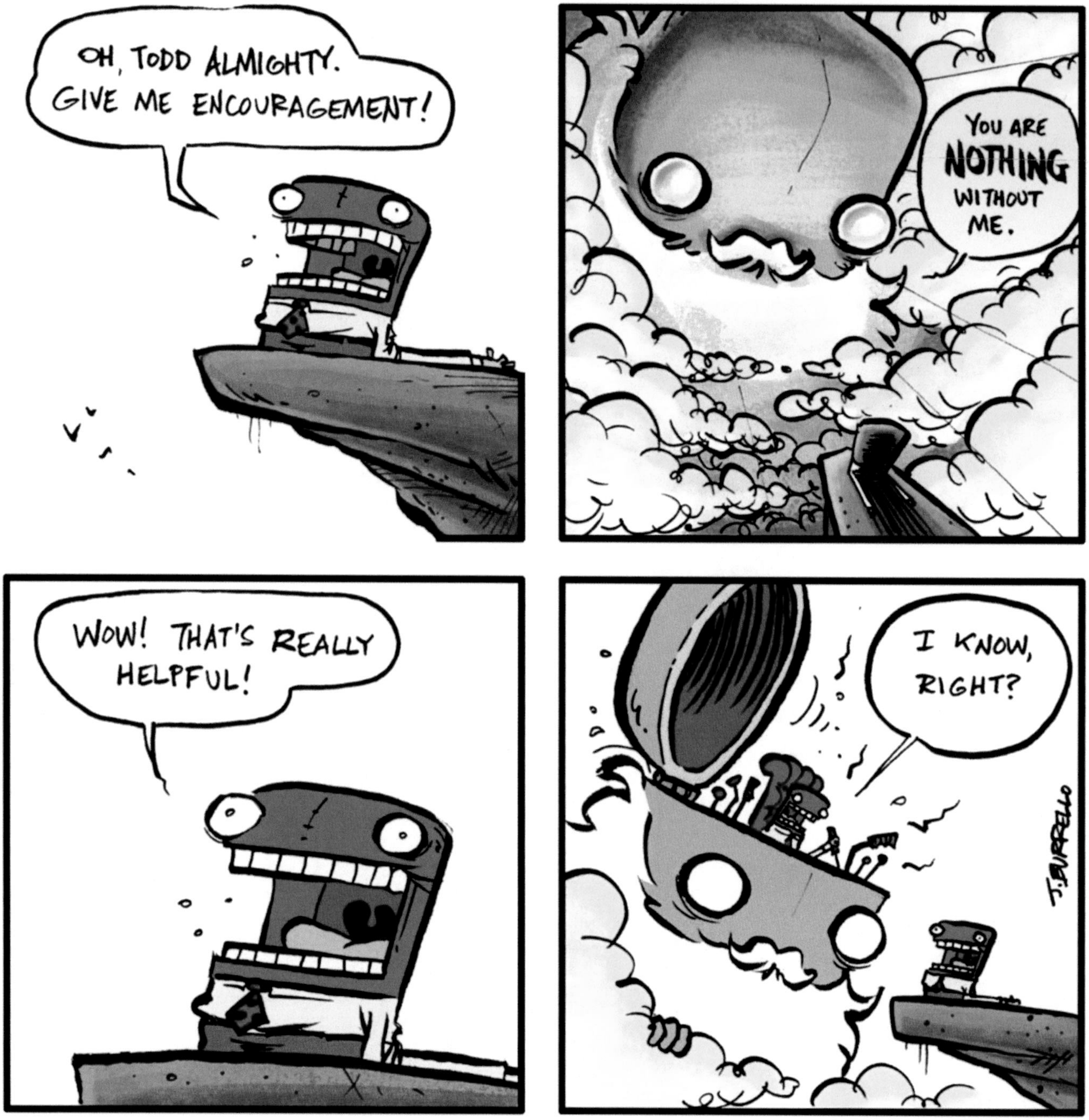
OH, TODD ALMIGHTY. GIVE ME ENCOURAGEMENT!
YOU ARE NOTHING WITHOUT ME.
WOW! THAT'S REALLY HELPFUL!
I KNOW, RIGHT?
J. BURRELLO

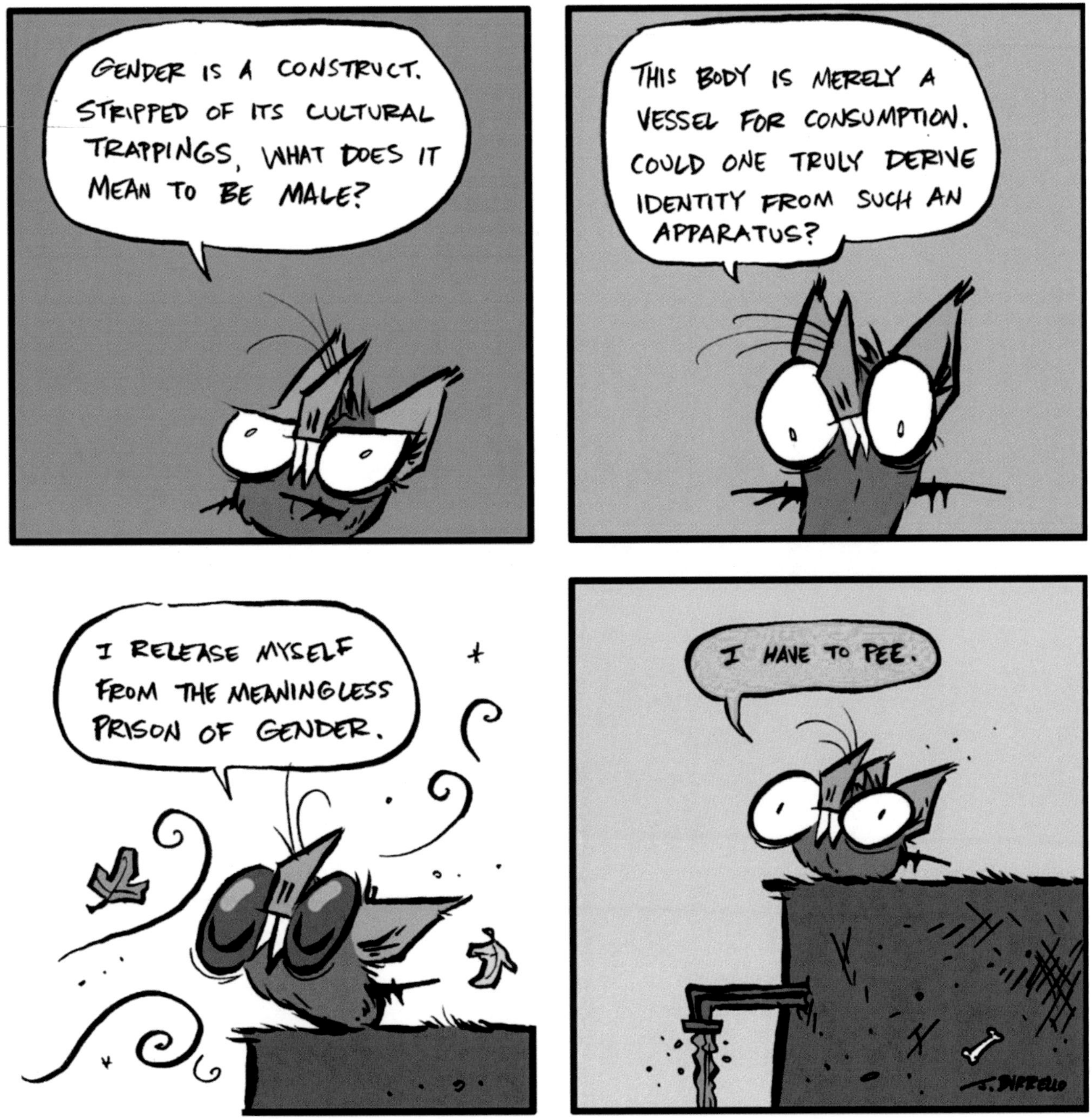
GENDER IS A CONSTRUCT. STRIPPED OF ITS CULTURAL TRAPPINGS, WHAT DOES IT MEAN TO BE MALE?
THIS BODY IS MERELY A VESSEL FOR CONSUMPTION. COULD ONE TRULY DERIVE IDENTITY FROM SUCH AN APPARATUS?
I RELEASE MYSELF FROM THE MEANINGLESS PRISON OF GENDER.
I HAVE TO PEE.

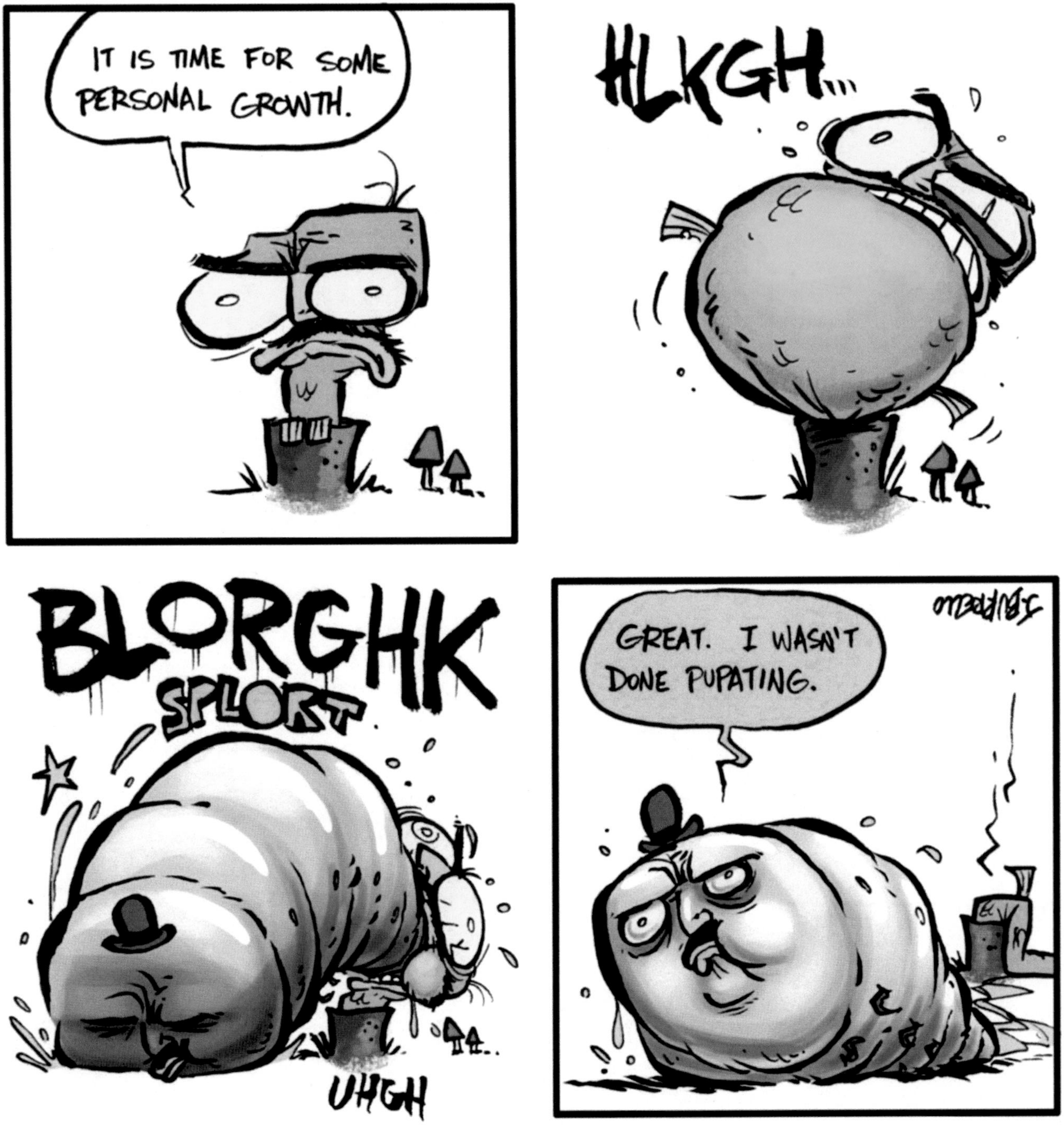
IT IS TIME FOR SOME PERSONAL GROWTH.
HLKGH...
BLORGHK
SPLORT
UHGH
GREAT. I WASN'T DONE PUPATING.

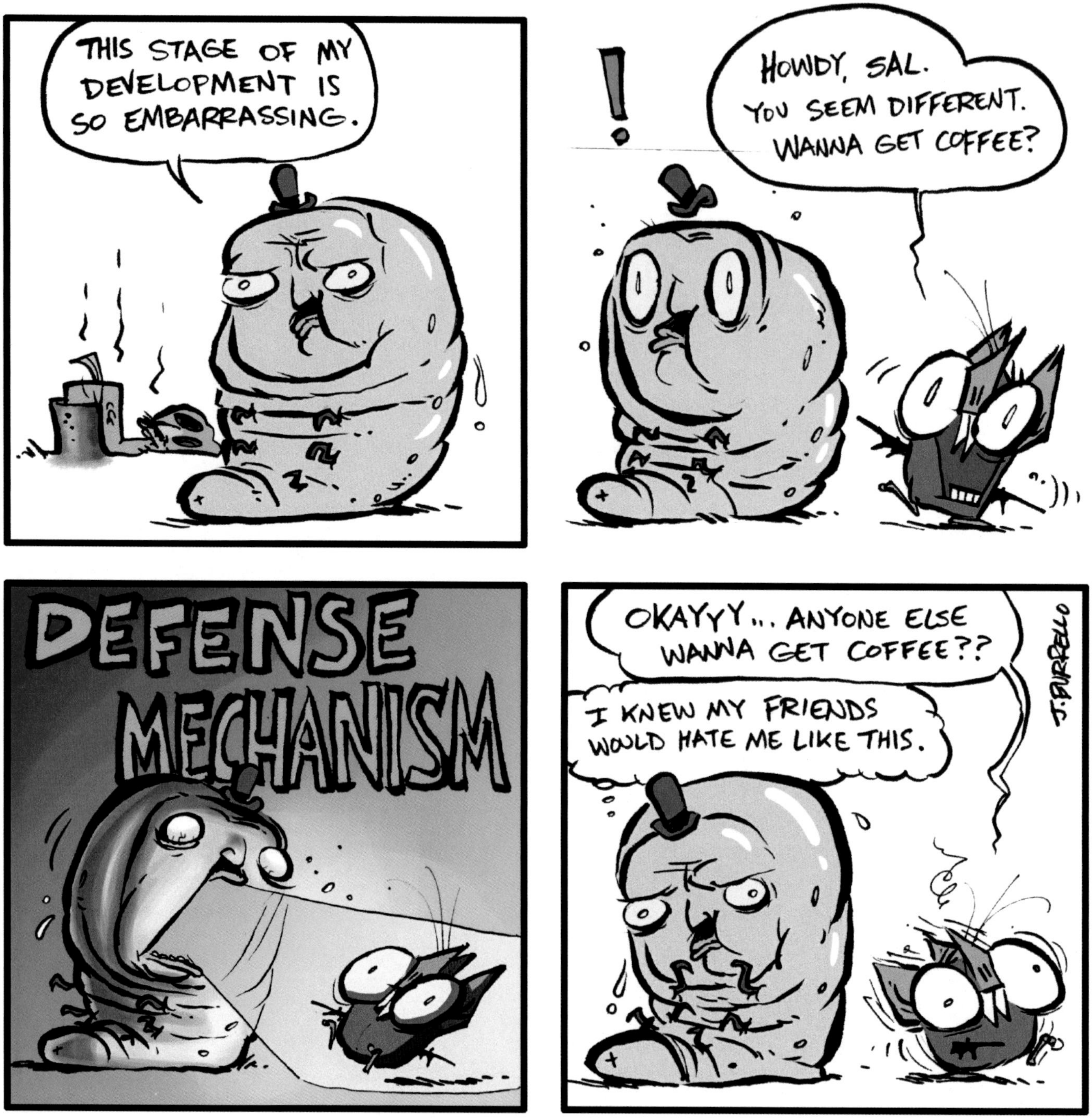
THIS STAGE OF MY DEVELOPMENT IS SO EMBARRASSING.
!
HOWDY, SAL. YOU SEEM DIFFERENT. WANNA GET COFFEE?
DEFENSE MECHANISM
OKAYYY... ANYONE ELSE WANNA GET COFFEE??
I KNEW MY FRIENDS WOULD HATE ME LIKE THIS.
J. BURRELLO

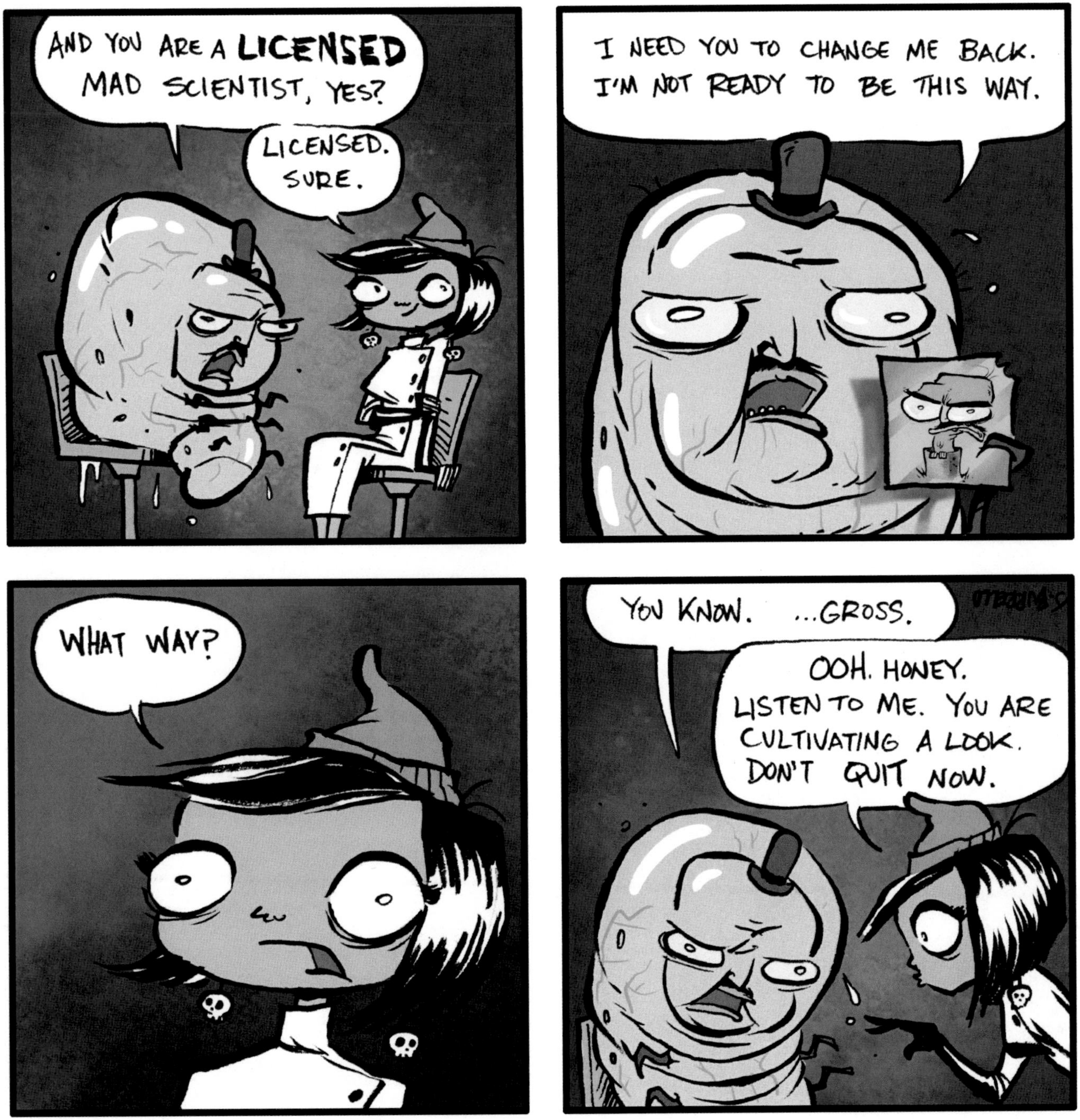
AND YOU ARE A **LICENSED** MAD SCIENTIST, YES?
LICENSED. SURE.
I NEED YOU TO CHANGE ME BACK. I'M NOT READY TO BE THIS WAY.
WHAT WAY?
YOU KNOW. ...GROSS.
OOH. HONEY. LISTEN TO ME. YOU ARE CULTIVATING A LOOK. DON'T QUIT NOW.

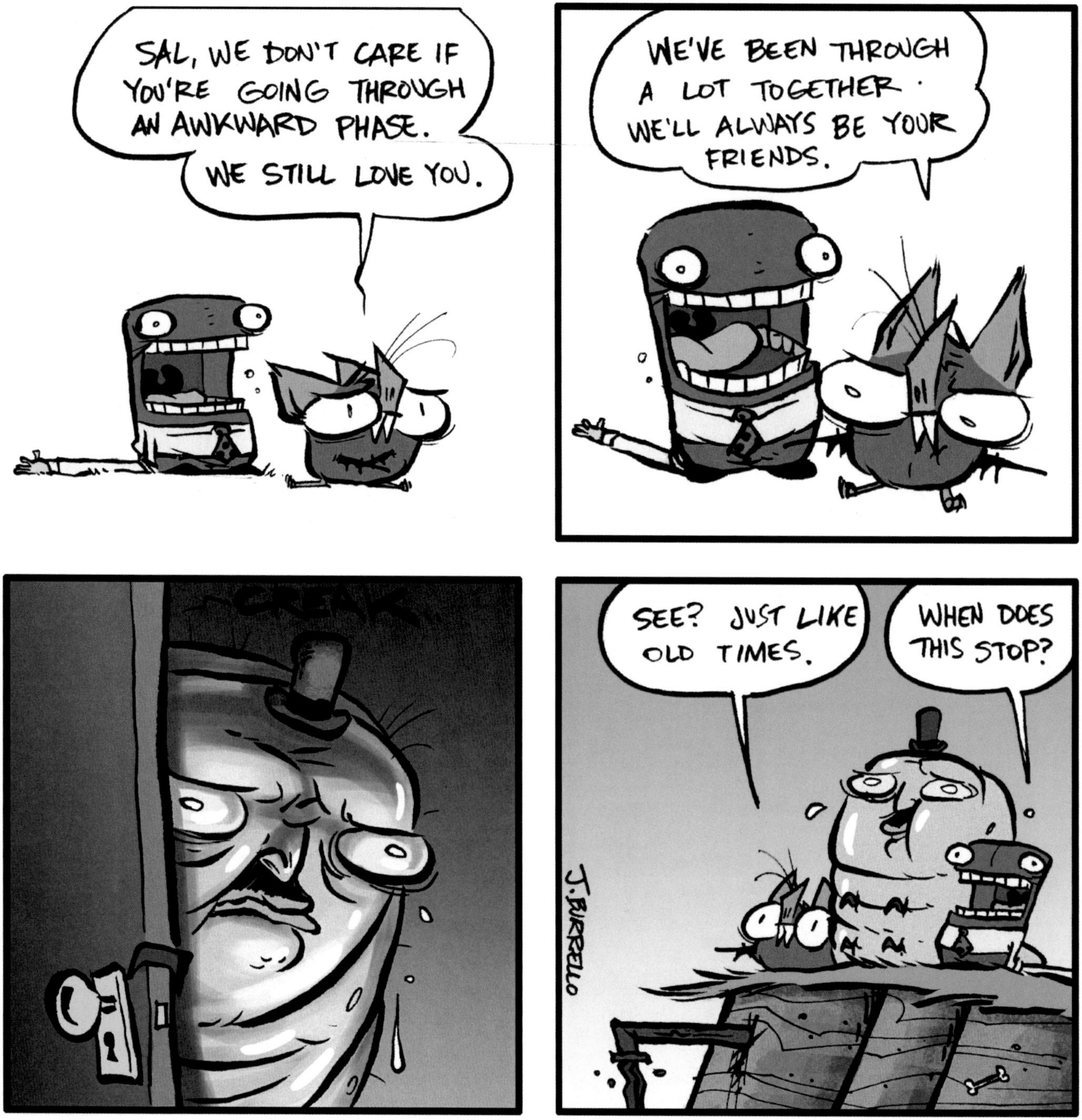
SAL, WE DON'T CARE IF YOU'RE GOING THROUGH AN AWKWARD PHASE.
WE STILL LOVE YOU.
WE'VE BEEN THROUGH A LOT TOGETHER. WE'LL ALWAYS BE YOUR FRIENDS.
CREAK
SEE? JUST LIKE OLD TIMES.
WHEN DOES THIS STOP?
J. BURRELLO

JEFF

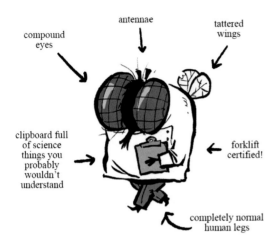

antennae

compound eyes

tattered wings

clipboard full of science things you probably wouldn't understand

forklift certified!

completely normal human legs

LUNA

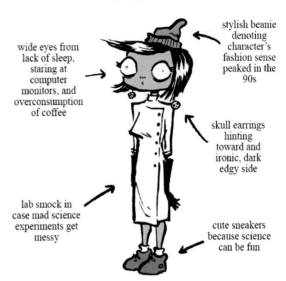

wide eyes from lack of sleep, staring at computer monitors, and overconsumption of coffee

stylish beanie denoting character's fashion sense peaked in the 90s

skull earrings hinting toward and ironic, dark edgy side

lab smock in case mad science experiments get messy

cute sneakers because science can be fun

BATHTUB BENNY

cherubic serenity

meatball sub

back hair

bathtub

can time travel

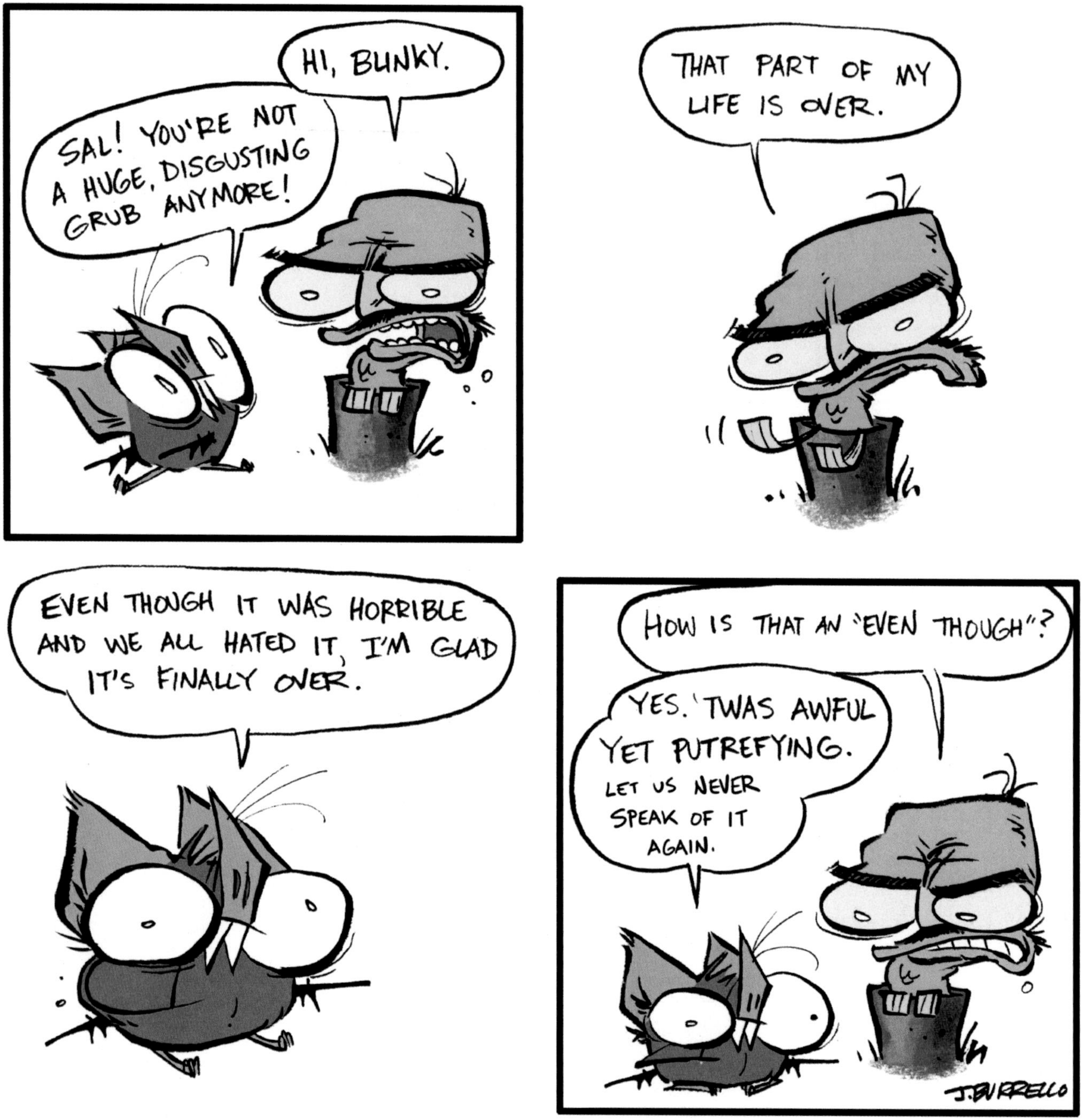
HI, BLINKY.
SAL! YOU'RE NOT A HUGE, DISGUSTING GRUB ANYMORE!
THAT PART OF MY LIFE IS OVER.
EVEN THOUGH IT WAS HORRIBLE AND WE ALL HATED IT, I'M GLAD IT'S FINALLY OVER.
HOW IS THAT AN "EVEN THOUGH"?
YES. 'TWAS AWFUL YET PUTREFYING.
LET US NEVER SPEAK OF IT AGAIN.
J.BURRELLO

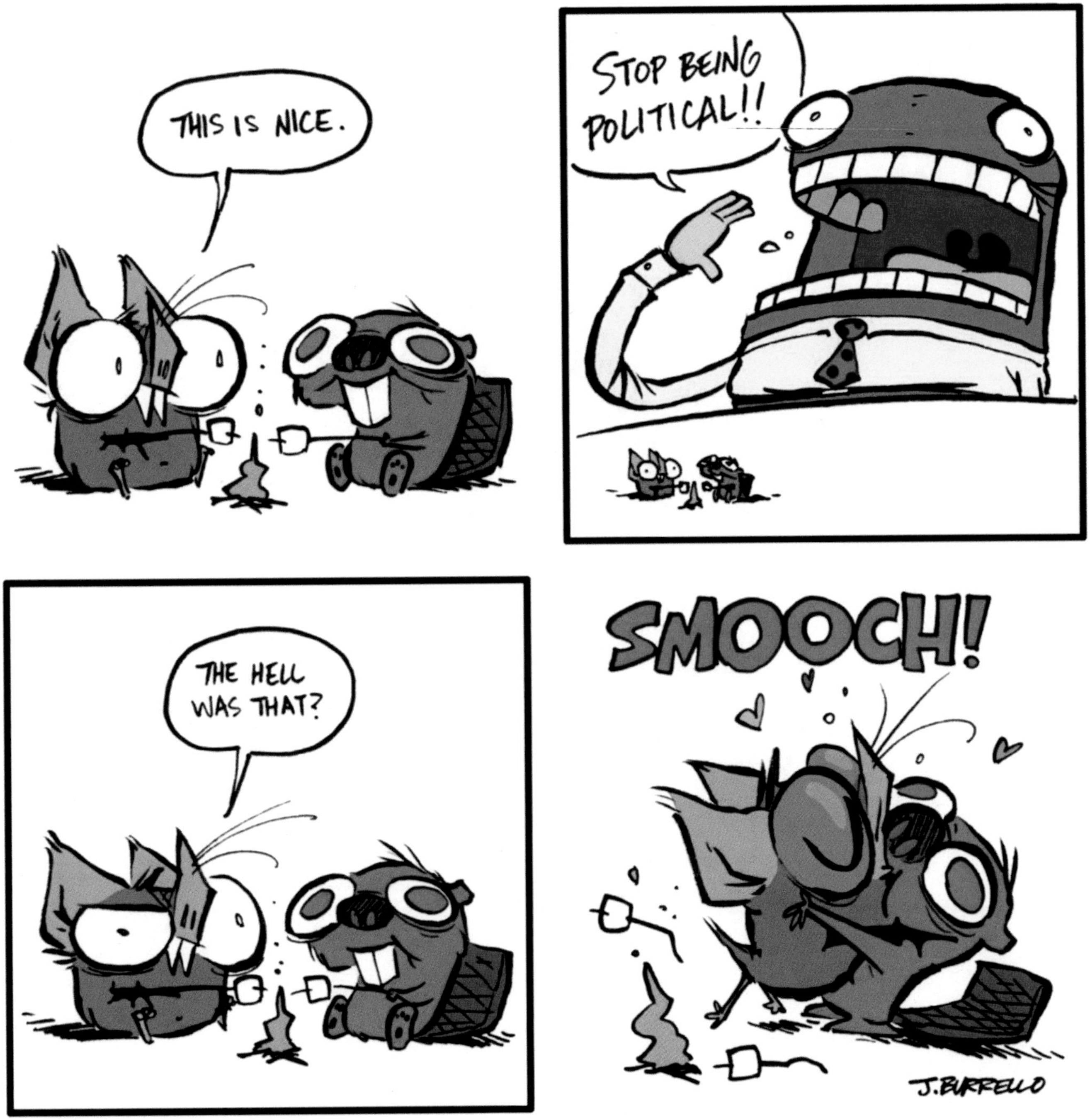
THIS IS NICE.
STOP BEING POLITICAL!!
THE HELL WAS THAT?
SMOOCH!
J.BURRELLO

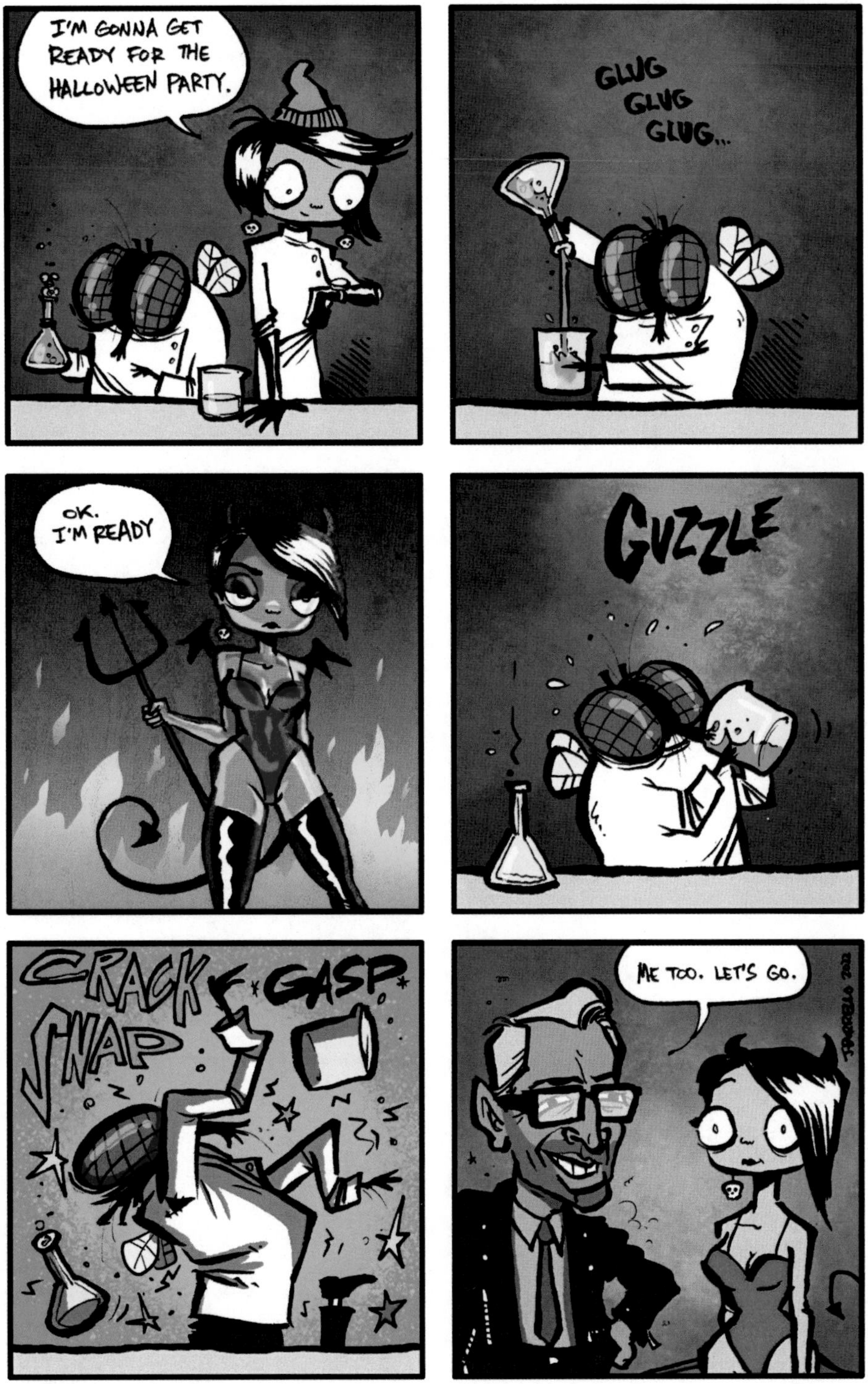
I'M GONNA GET READY FOR THE HALLOWEEN PARTY.
GLUG GLUG GLUG...
OK. I'M READY
GUZZLE
CRACK
GASP
SNAP
ME TOO. LET'S GO.

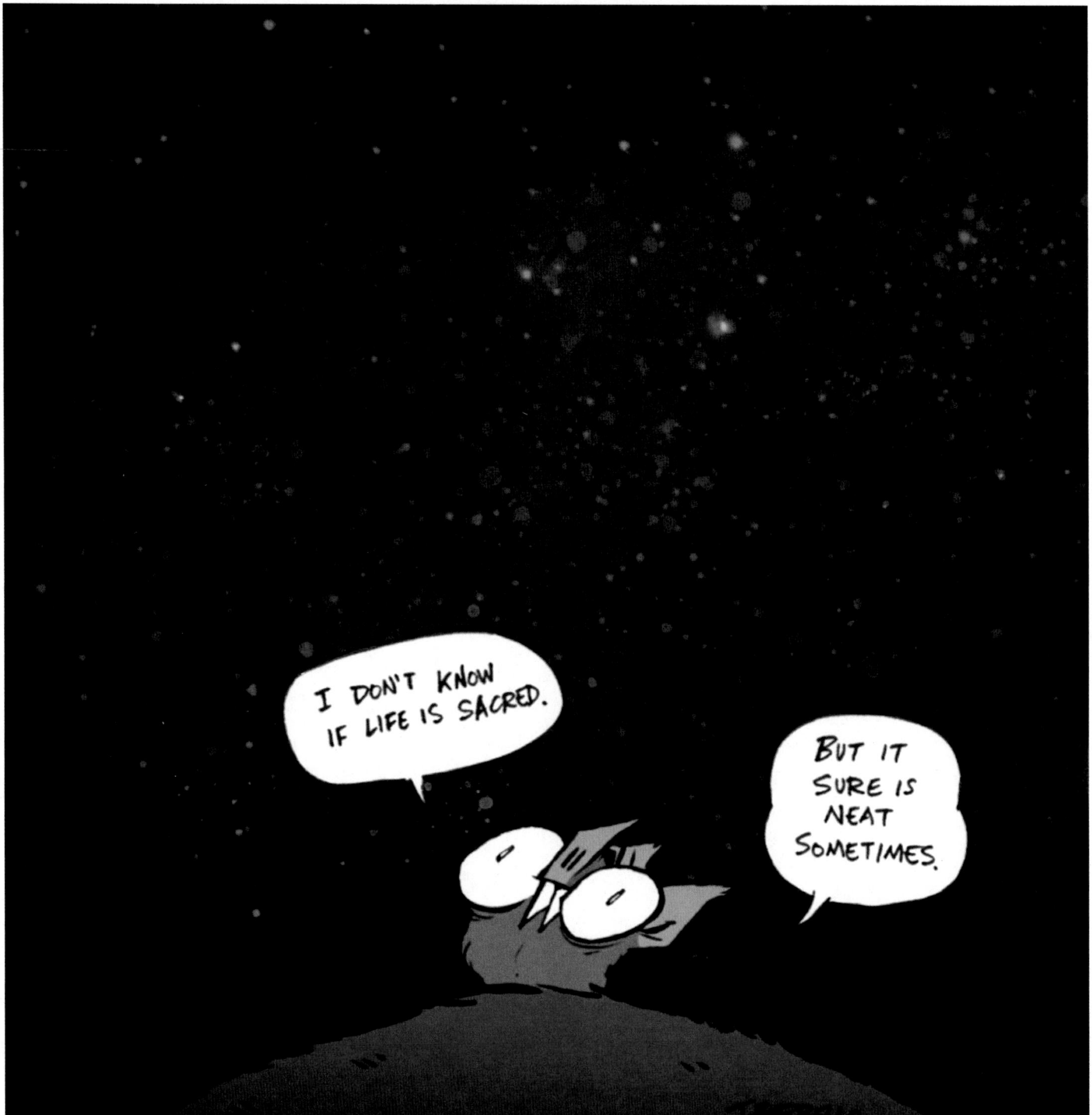
I DON'T KNOW IF LIFE IS SACRED.
BUT IT SURE IS NEAT SOMETIMES.

Elevator Music

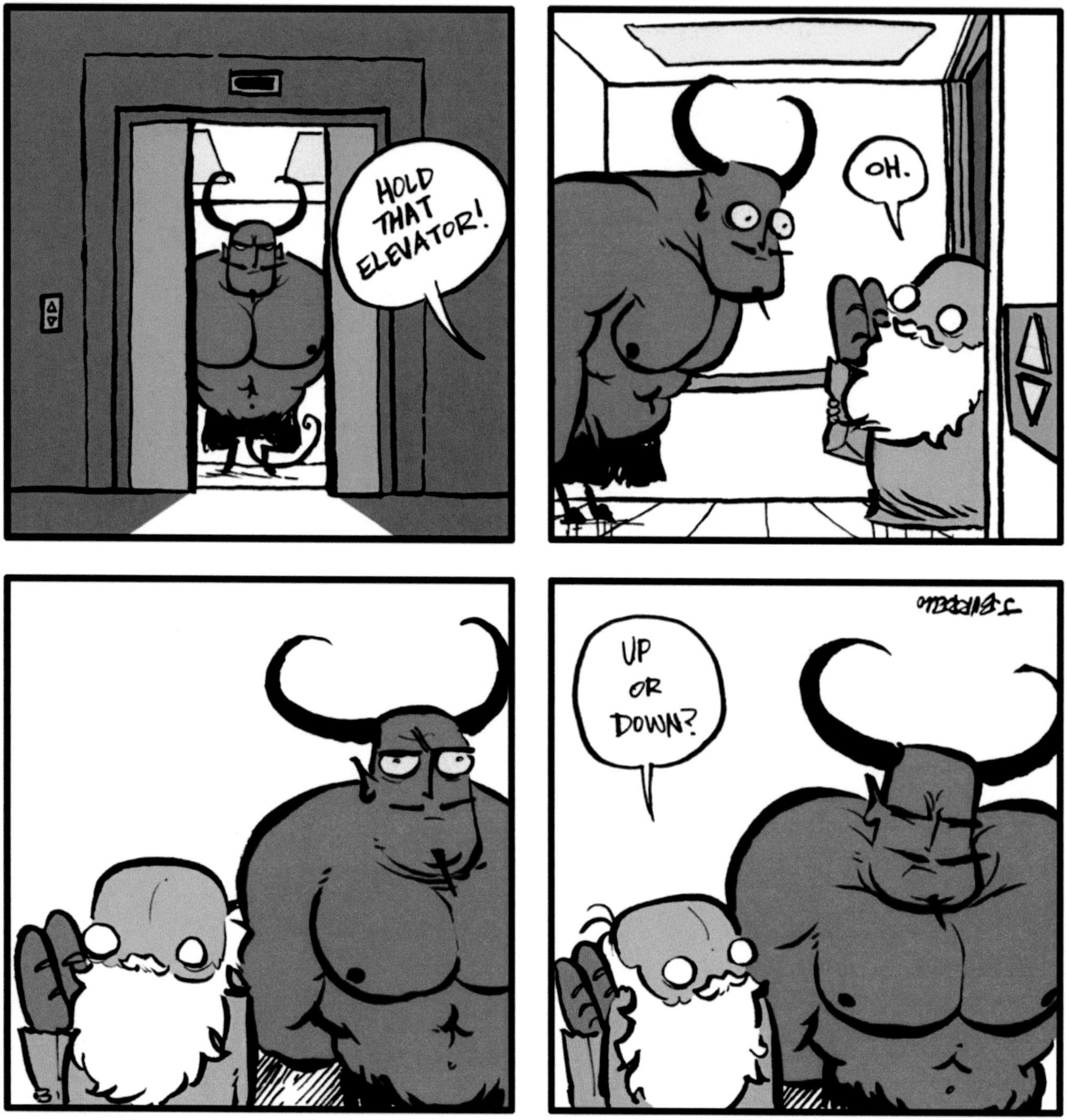
HOLD THAT ELEVATOR!
OH.
UP OR DOWN?

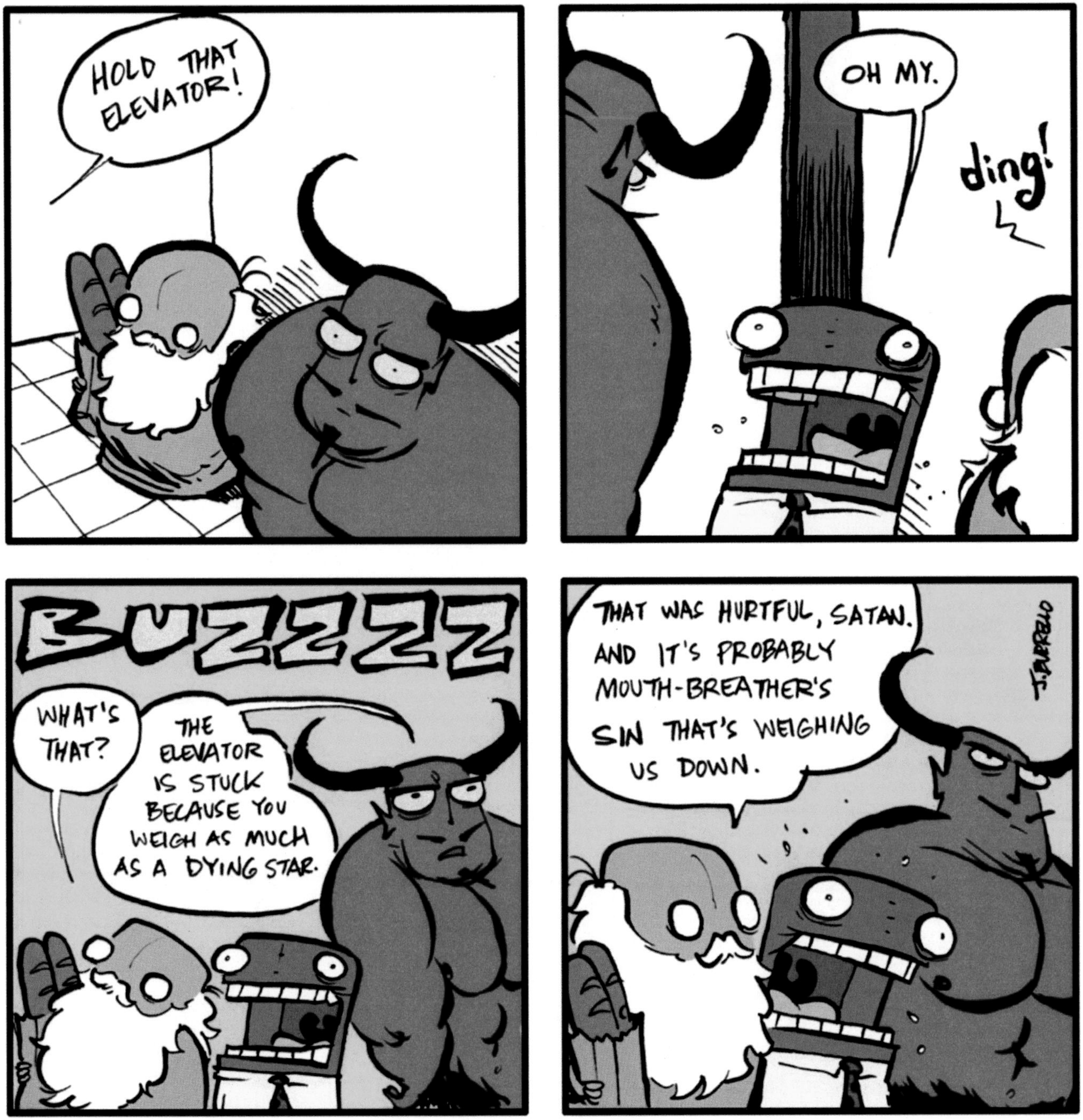
HOLD THAT ELEVATOR!
OH MY.
ding!
BUZZZZZ
WHAT'S THAT?
THE ELEVATOR IS STUCK BECAUSE YOU WEIGH AS MUCH AS A DYING STAR.
THAT WAS HURTFUL, SATAN. AND IT'S PROBABLY MOUTH-BREATHER'S SIN THAT'S WEIGHING US DOWN.
J. BARBELLO

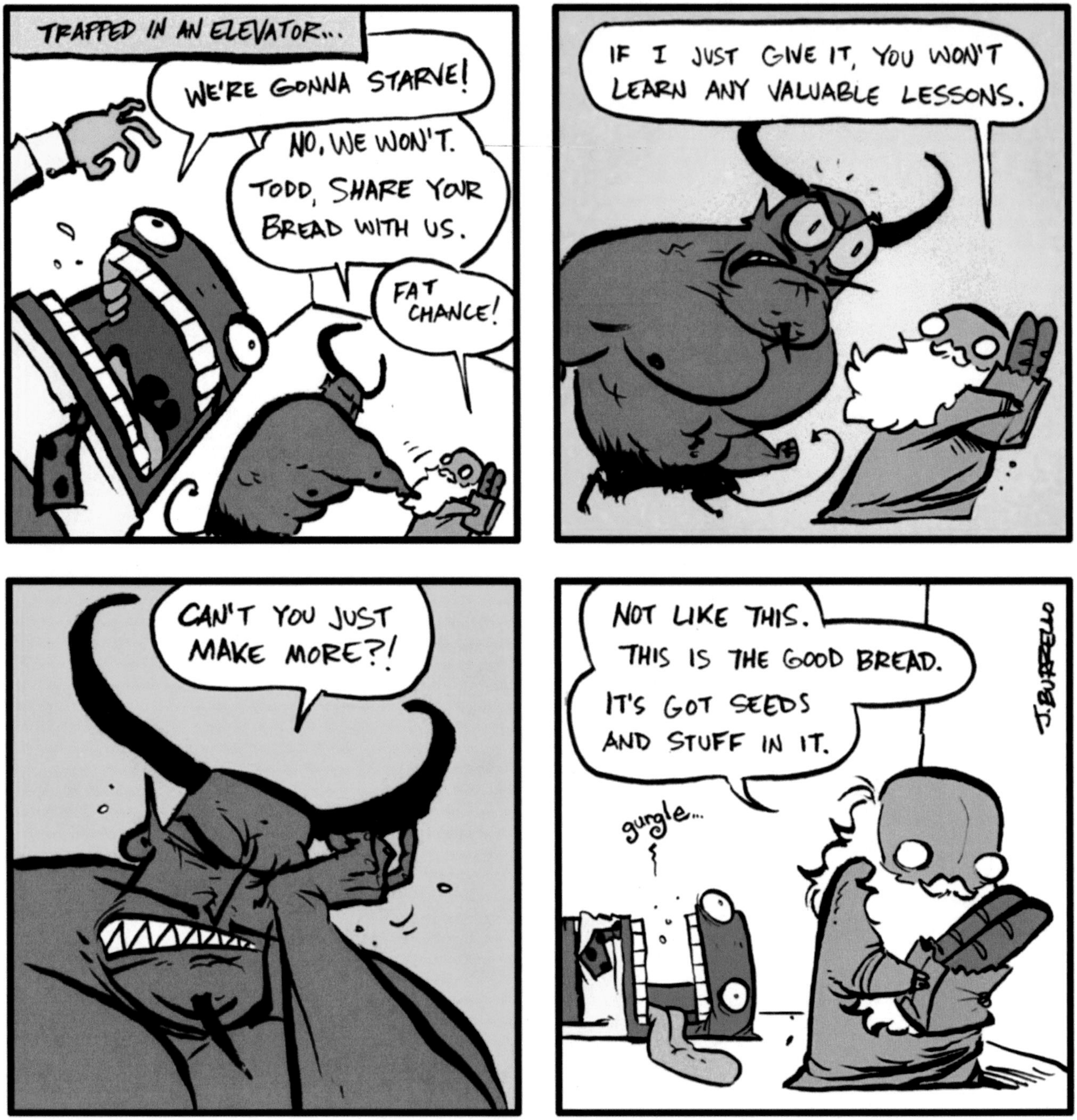
TRAPPED IN AN ELEVATOR...
WE'RE GONNA STARVE!
NO, WE WON'T.
TODD, SHARE YOUR BREAD WITH US.
FAT CHANCE!
IF I JUST GIVE IT, YOU WON'T LEARN ANY VALUABLE LESSONS.
CAN'T YOU JUST MAKE MORE?!
NOT LIKE THIS.
THIS IS THE GOOD BREAD.
IT'S GOT SEEDS AND STUFF IN IT.
gurgle...
J. BURRELLO

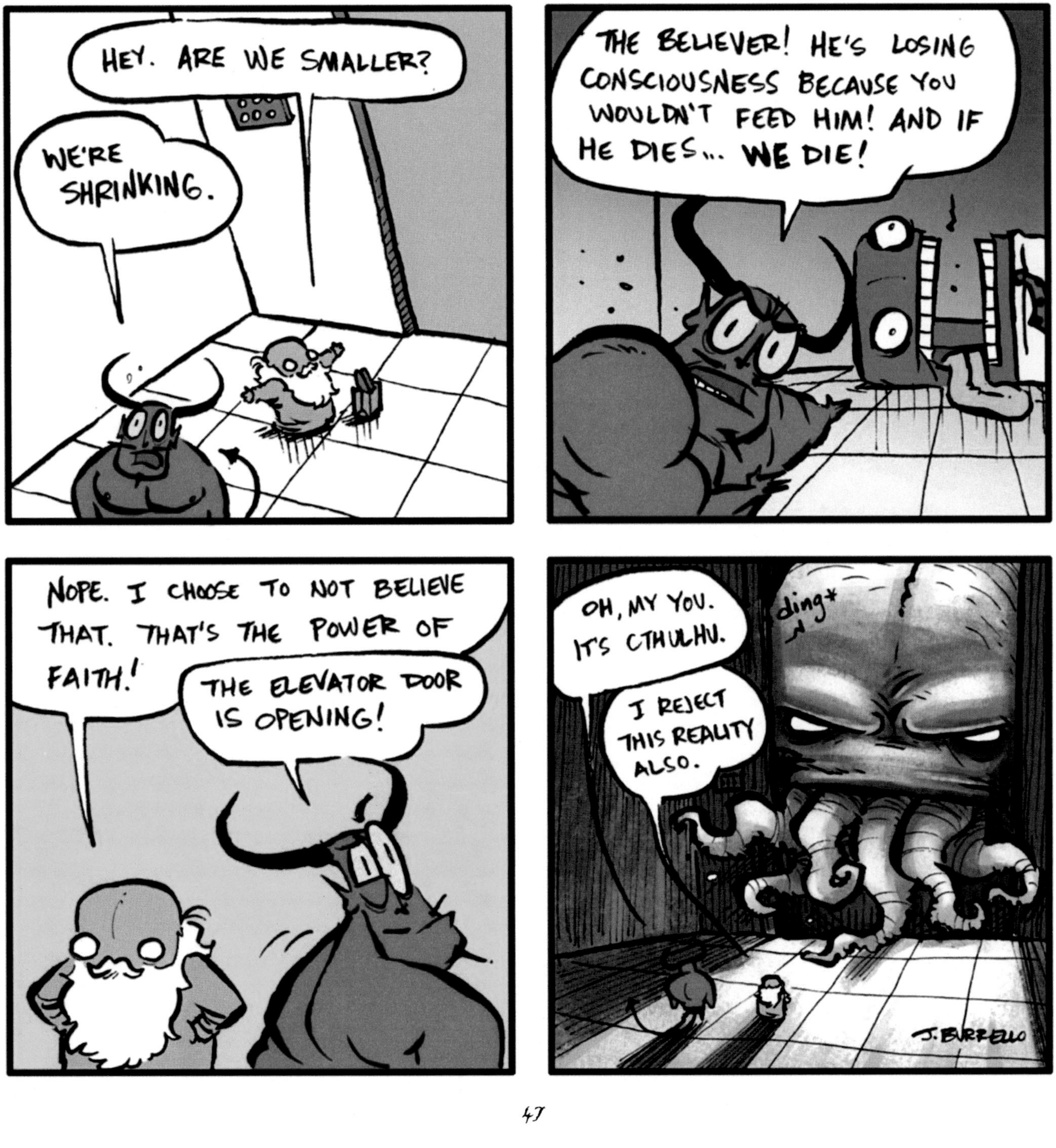
HEY. ARE WE SMALLER?
WE'RE SHRINKING.
THE BELIEVER! HE'S LOSING CONSCIOUSNESS BECAUSE YOU WOULDN'T FEED HIM! AND IF HE DIES... WE DIE!
NOPE. I CHOOSE TO NOT BELIEVE THAT. THAT'S THE POWER OF FAITH!
THE ELEVATOR DOOR IS OPENING!
ding*
OH, MY YOU. IT'S CTHULHU.
I REJECT THIS REALITY ALSO.
J. BURRELLO

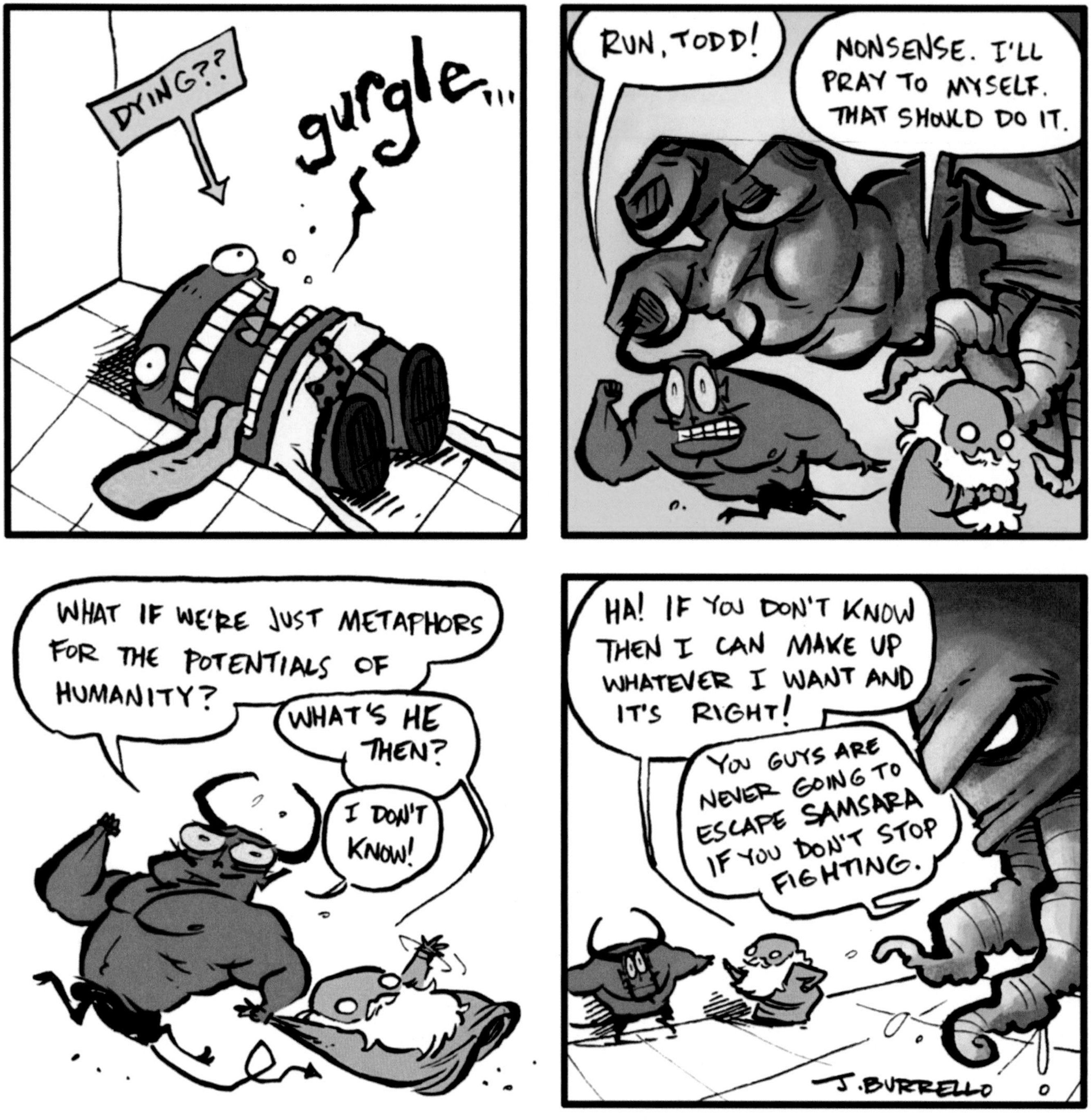
DYING??
gurgle...
RUN, TODD!
NONSENSE. I'LL PRAY TO MYSELF. THAT SHOULD DO IT.
WHAT IF WE'RE JUST METAPHORS FOR THE POTENTIALS OF HUMANITY?
WHAT'S HE THEN?
I DON'T KNOW!
HA! IF YOU DON'T KNOW THEN I CAN MAKE UP WHATEVER I WANT AND IT'S RIGHT!
YOU GUYS ARE NEVER GOING TO ESCAPE SAMSARA IF YOU DON'T STOP FIGHTING.
J. BURRELLO

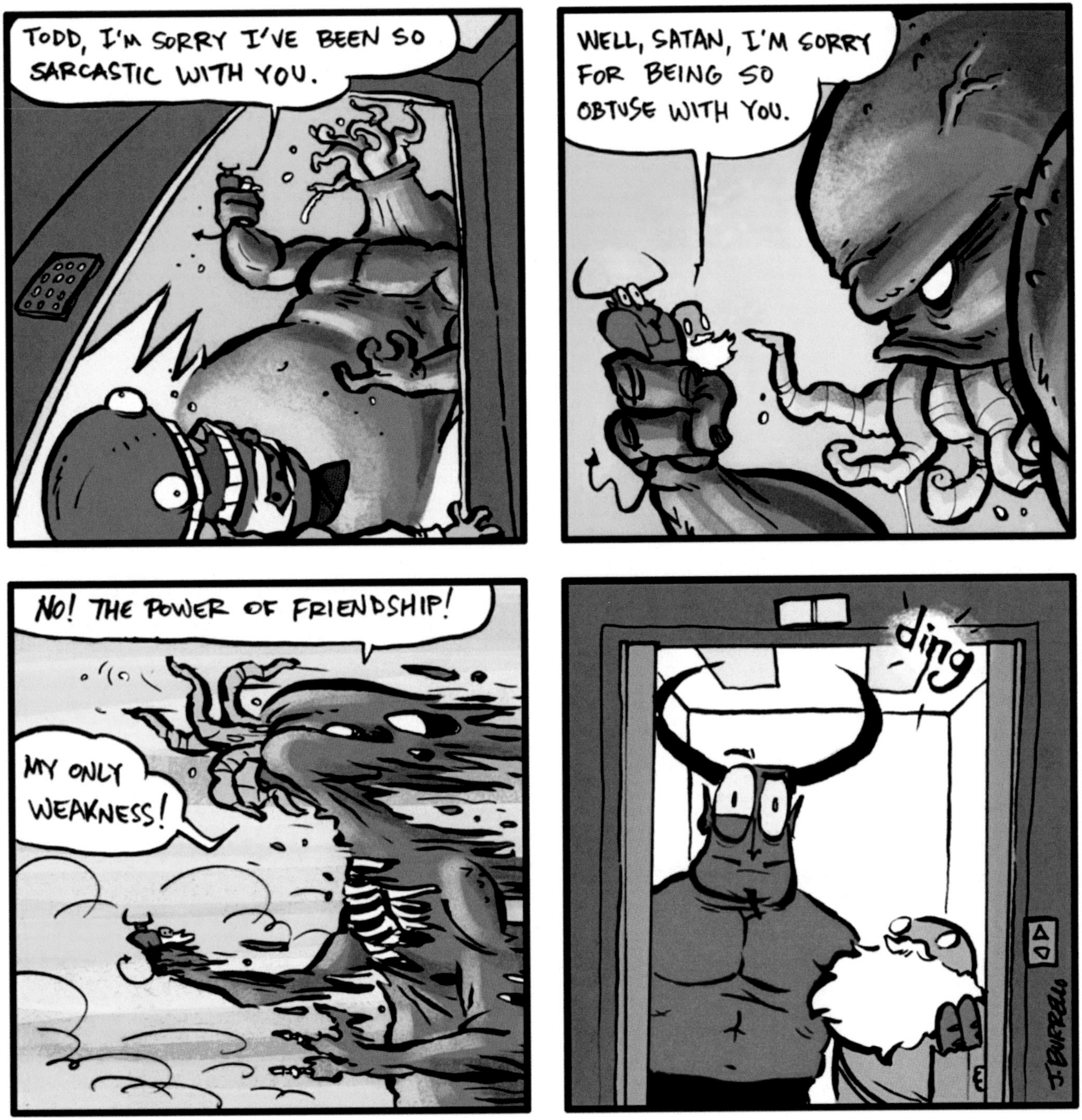
TODD, I'M SORRY I'VE BEEN SO SARCASTIC WITH YOU.
WELL, SATAN, I'M SORRY FOR BEING SO OBTUSE WITH YOU.
NO! THE POWER OF FRIENDSHIP!
MY ONLY WEAKNESS!
ding
J. BUFFELLI

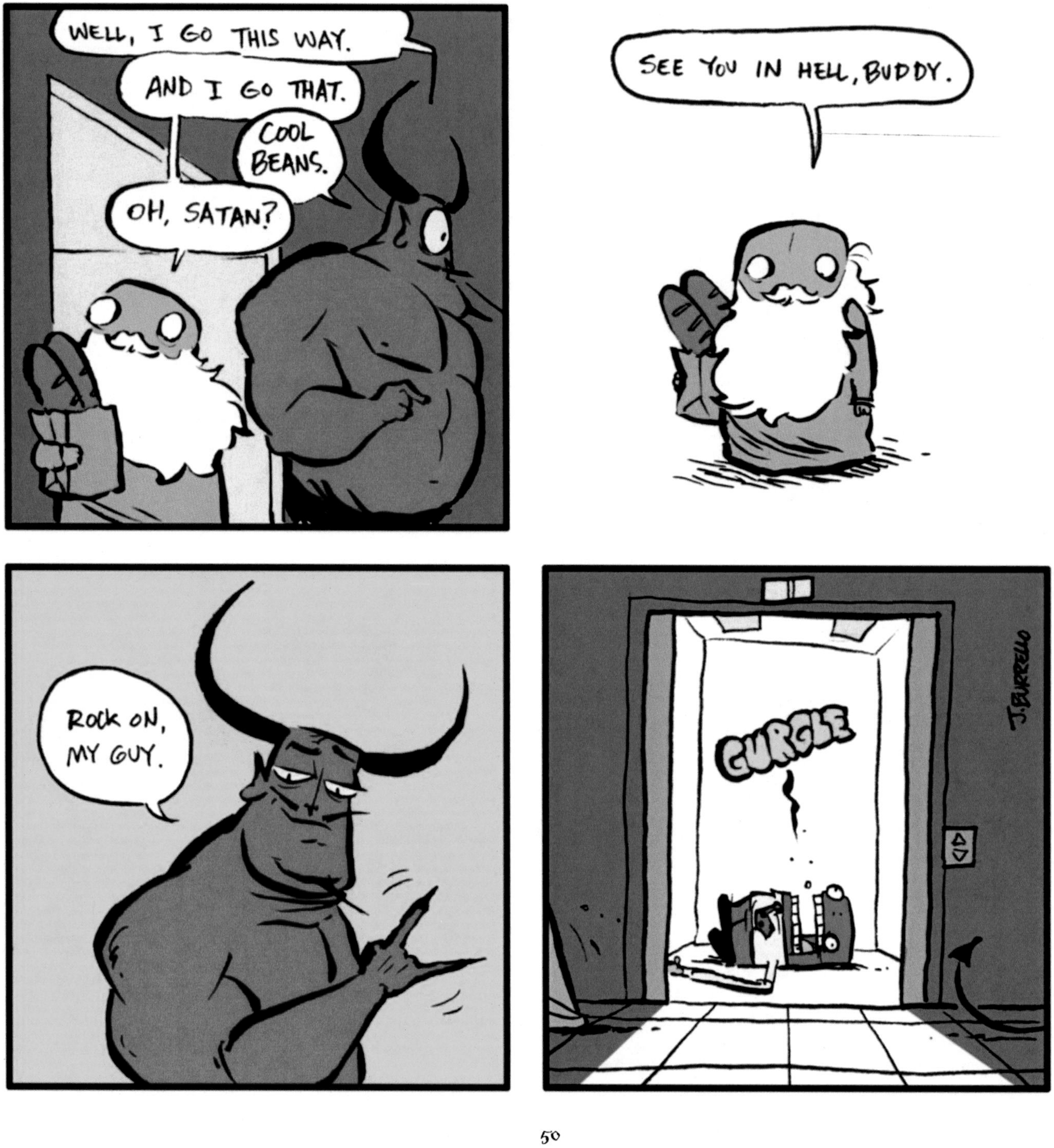
WELL, I GO THIS WAY.
AND I GO THAT.
COOL BEANS.
OH, SATAN?
SEE YOU IN HELL, BUDDY.
ROCK ON, MY GUY.
GURGLE
J. BURRELLO

TODD

empty eyes that can shoot laser beams I bet

bald.
Not having hair is not only fine, but holy maybe or something

nice, white, fluffy, woolly beard that belies the nightmarish reality that he has no lips and just scary, weird teeth under there

stylish robe that has never been washed because soap is evil

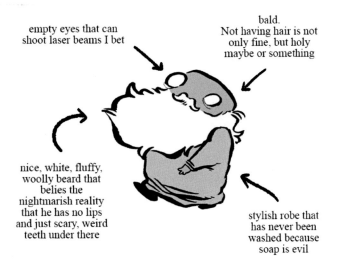

SATAN

compacted keratin

magnificent upper body strength (probably abusing steroids)

embarrassing, outmoded jazz musician facial hair configuration

looks like somebody skipped leg day

classic pointy tail

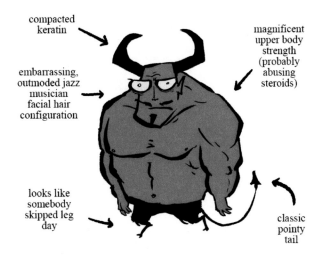

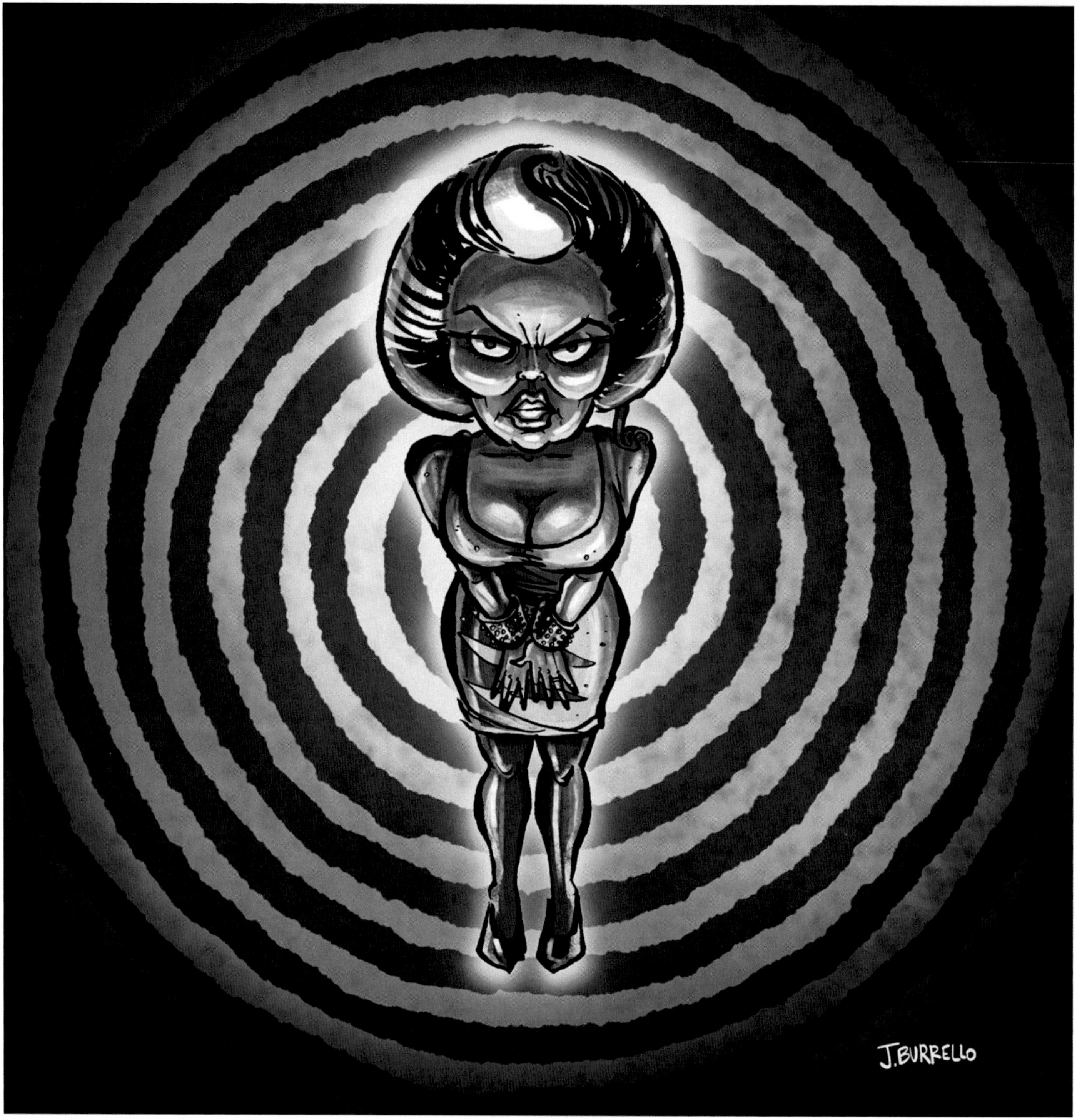
J.BURRELLO

HAUNTED SAFARI

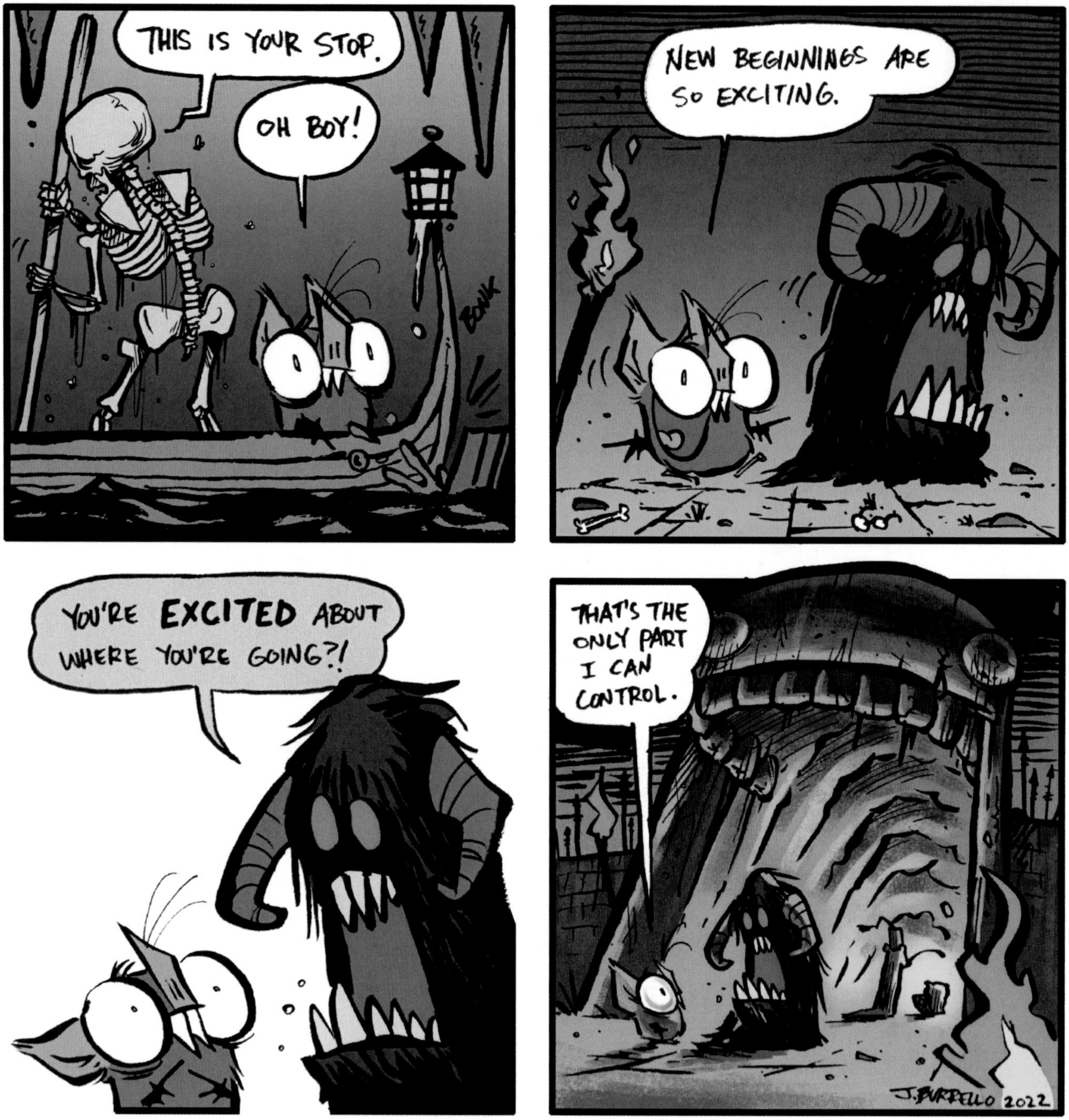
THIS IS YOUR STOP.
OH BOY!
BONK
NEW BEGINNINGS ARE SO EXCITING.
YOU'RE **EXCITED** ABOUT WHERE YOU'RE GOING?!
THAT'S THE ONLY PART I CAN CONTROL.
J. BURRELLO 2022

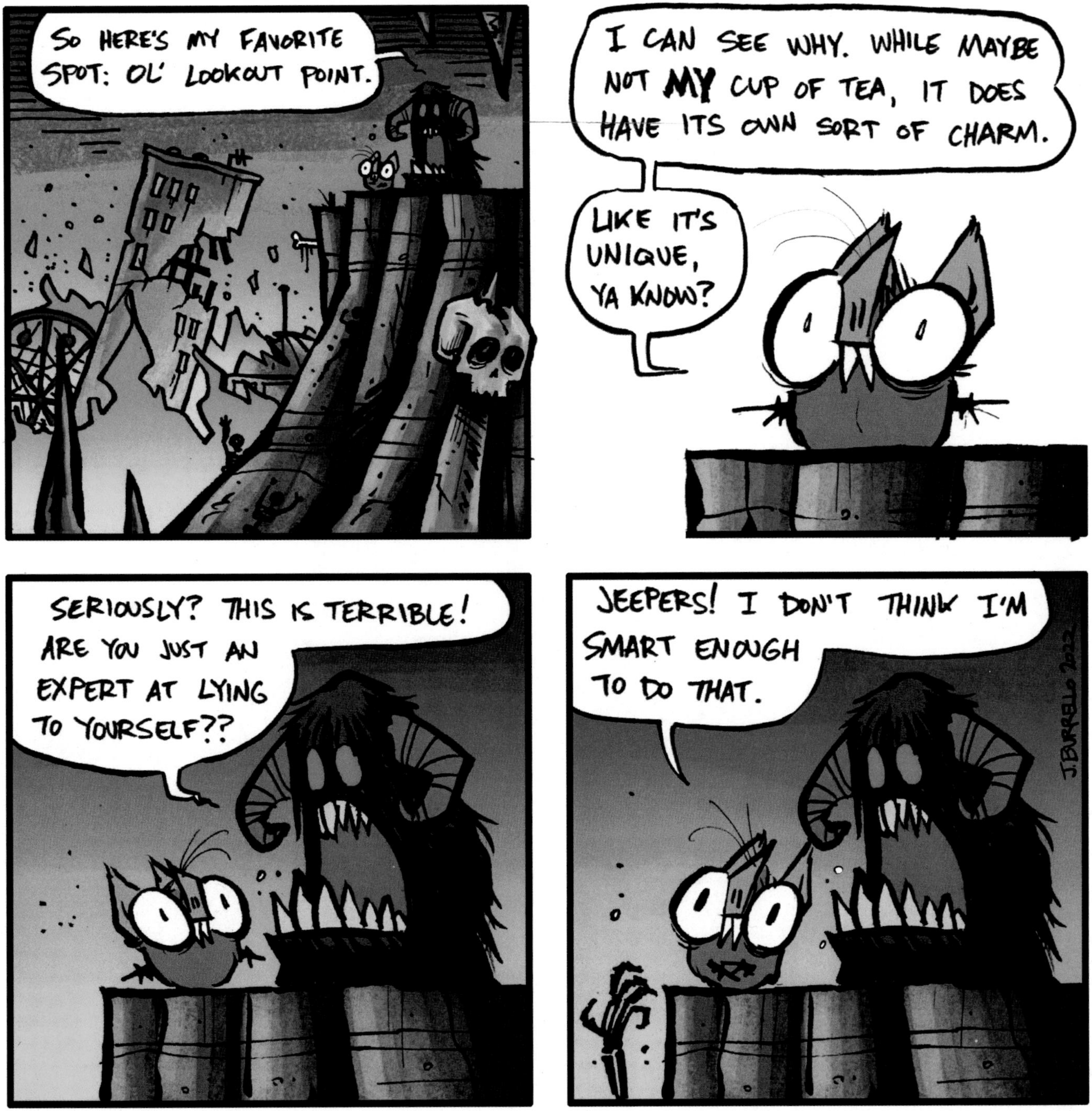
SO HERE'S MY FAVORITE SPOT: OL' LOOKOUT POINT.
I CAN SEE WHY. WHILE MAYBE NOT MY CUP OF TEA, IT DOES HAVE ITS OWN SORT OF CHARM.
LIKE IT'S UNIQUE, YA KNOW?
SERIOUSLY? THIS IS TERRIBLE! ARE YOU JUST AN EXPERT AT LYING TO YOURSELF??
JEEPERS! I DON'T THINK I'M SMART ENOUGH TO DO THAT.
J.BURRELLO 2022

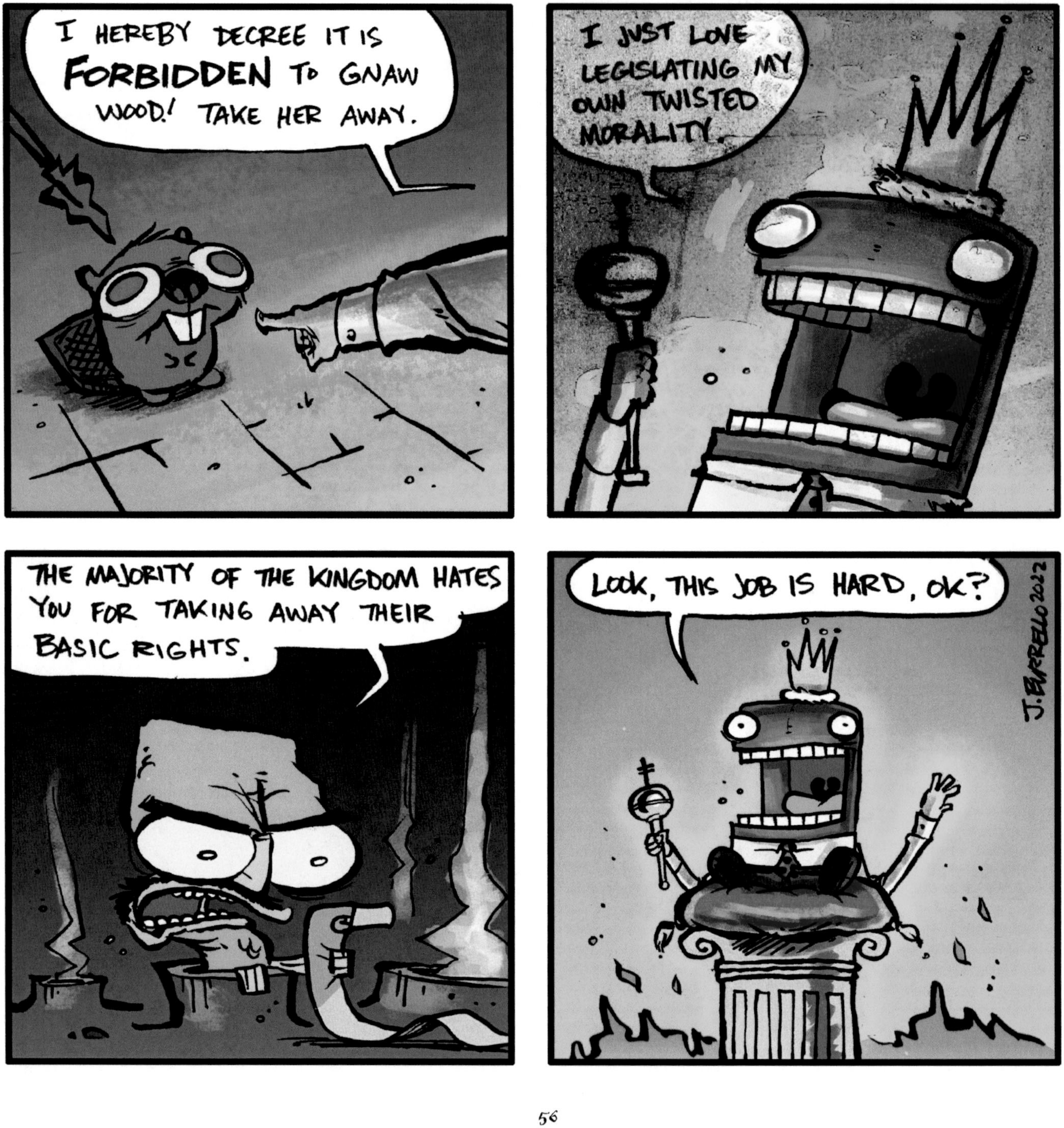
I HEREBY DECREE IT IS FORBIDDEN TO GNAW WOOD! TAKE HER AWAY.
I JUST LOVE LEGISLATING MY OWN TWISTED MORALITY.
THE MAJORITY OF THE KINGDOM HATES YOU FOR TAKING AWAY THEIR BASIC RIGHTS.
LOOK, THIS JOB IS HARD, OK?
J. BARRELLO 2022

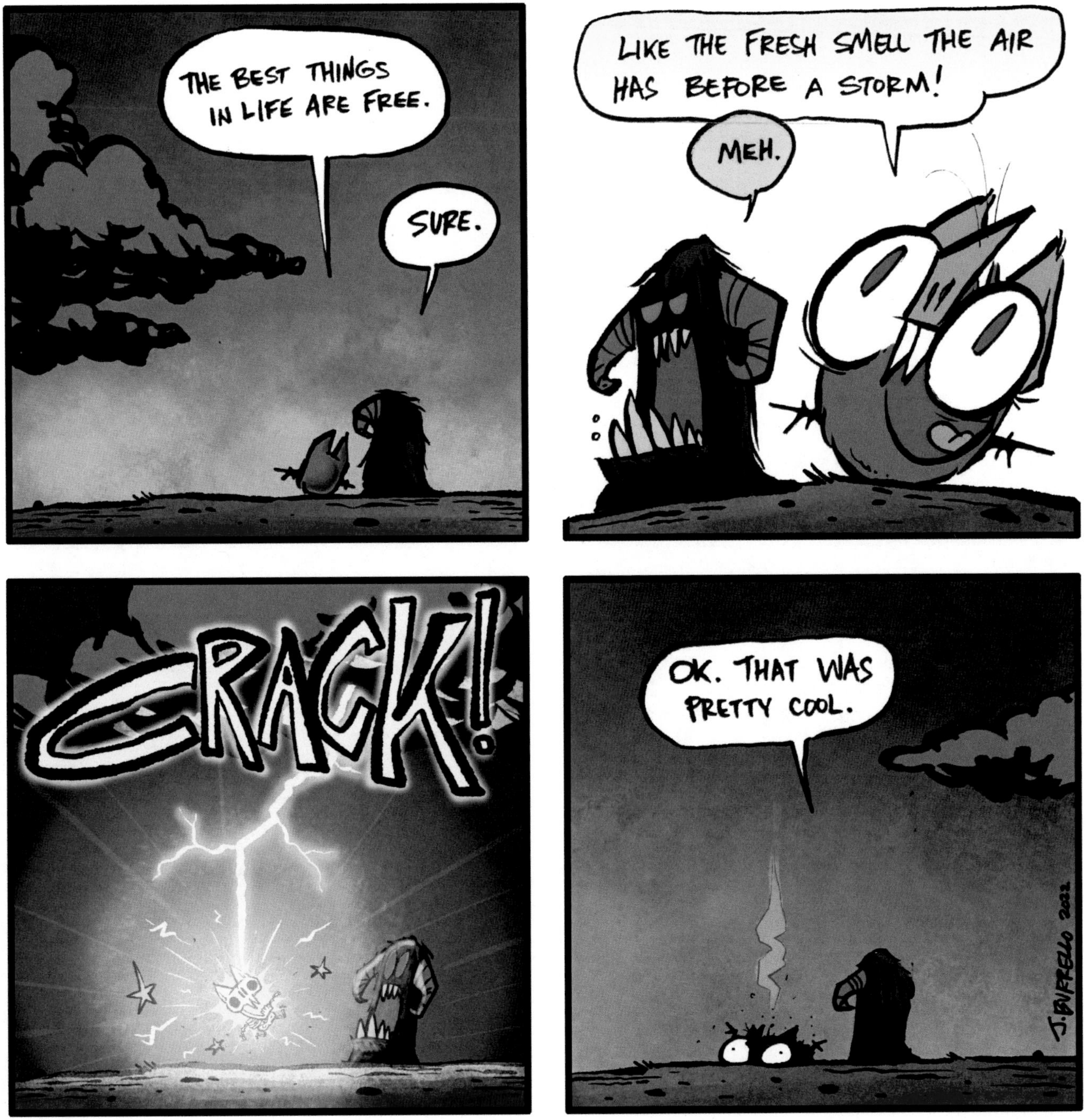
THE BEST THINGS IN LIFE ARE FREE.
SURE.
LIKE THE FRESH SMELL THE AIR HAS BEFORE A STORM!
MEH.
CRACK!
OK. THAT WAS PRETTY COOL.
J. BUFFELLO 2022

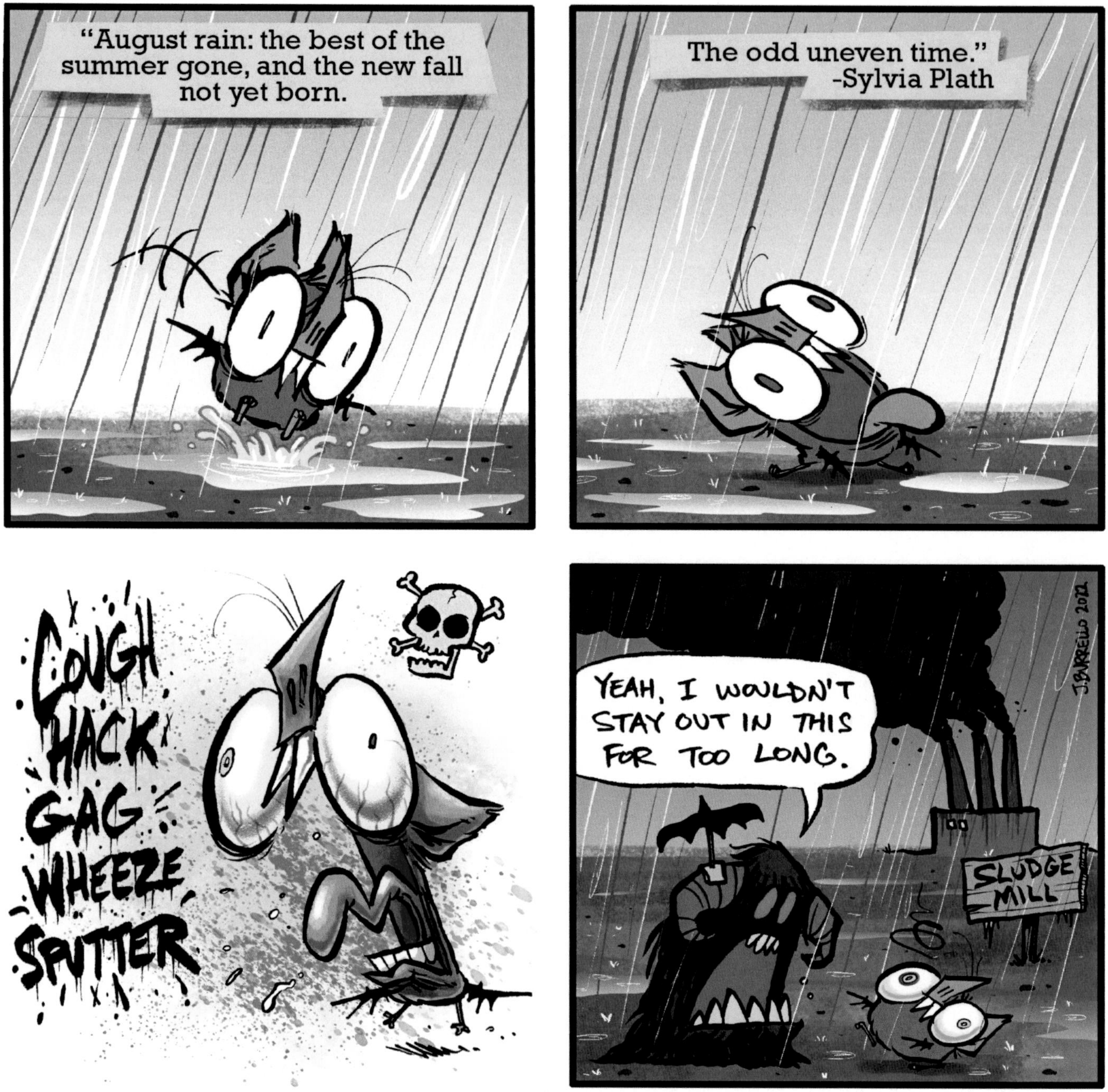
"August rain: the best of the summer gone, and the new fall not yet born.
The odd uneven time."
-Sylvia Plath
COUGH
HACK
GAG
WHEEZE
SPUTTER
J.BURRELLO 2012
YEAH, I WOULDN'T STAY OUT IN THIS FOR TOO LONG.
SLUDGE MILL

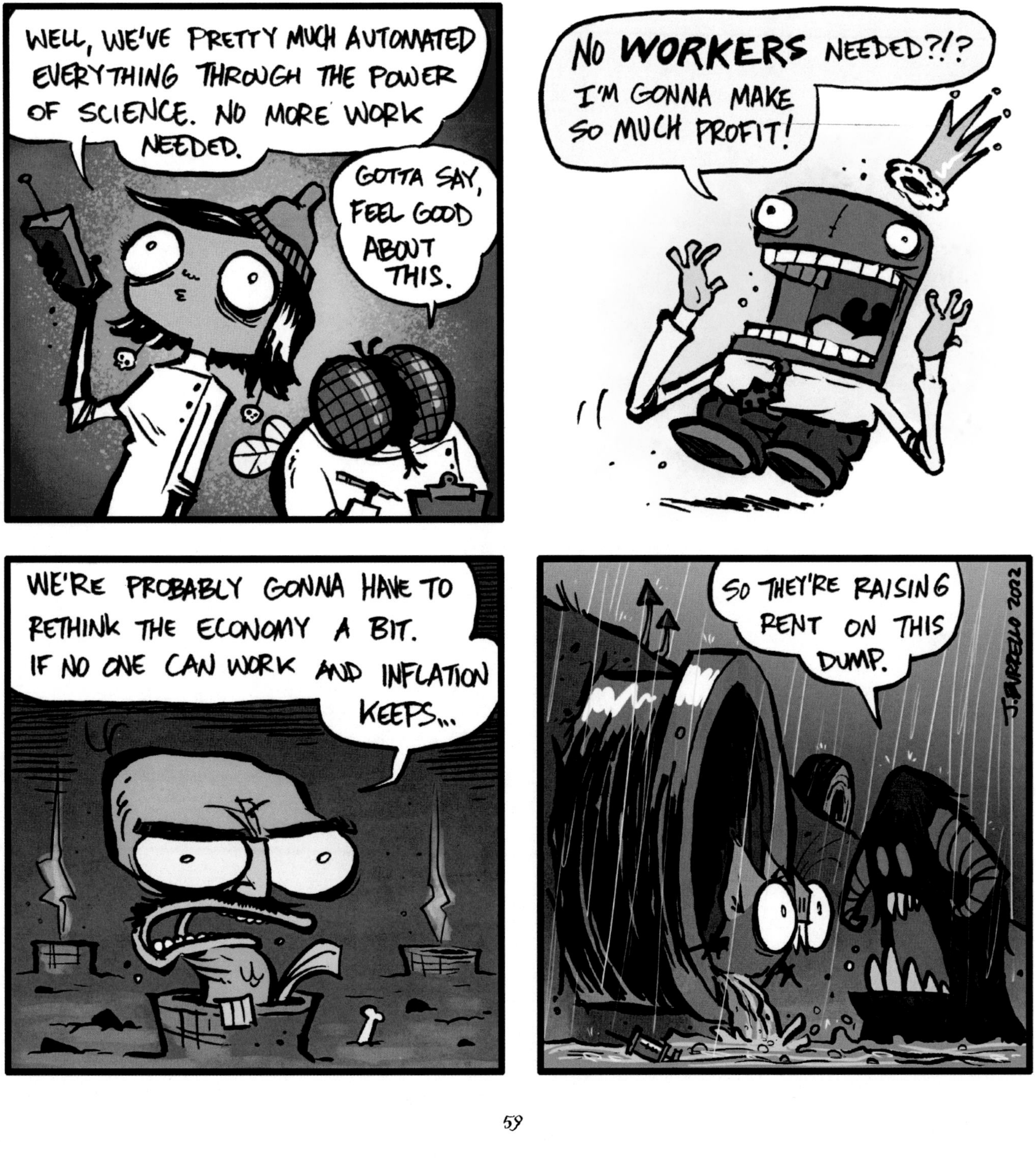
WELL, WE'VE PRETTY MUCH AUTOMATED EVERYTHING THROUGH THE POWER OF SCIENCE. NO MORE WORK NEEDED.
GOTTA SAY, FEEL GOOD ABOUT THIS.
NO WORKERS NEEDED?!? I'M GONNA MAKE SO MUCH PROFIT!
WE'RE PROBABLY GONNA HAVE TO RETHINK THE ECONOMY A BIT. IF NO ONE CAN WORK AND INFLATION KEEPS...
SO THEY'RE RAISING RENT ON THIS DUMP.
J. BURRELLO 2022

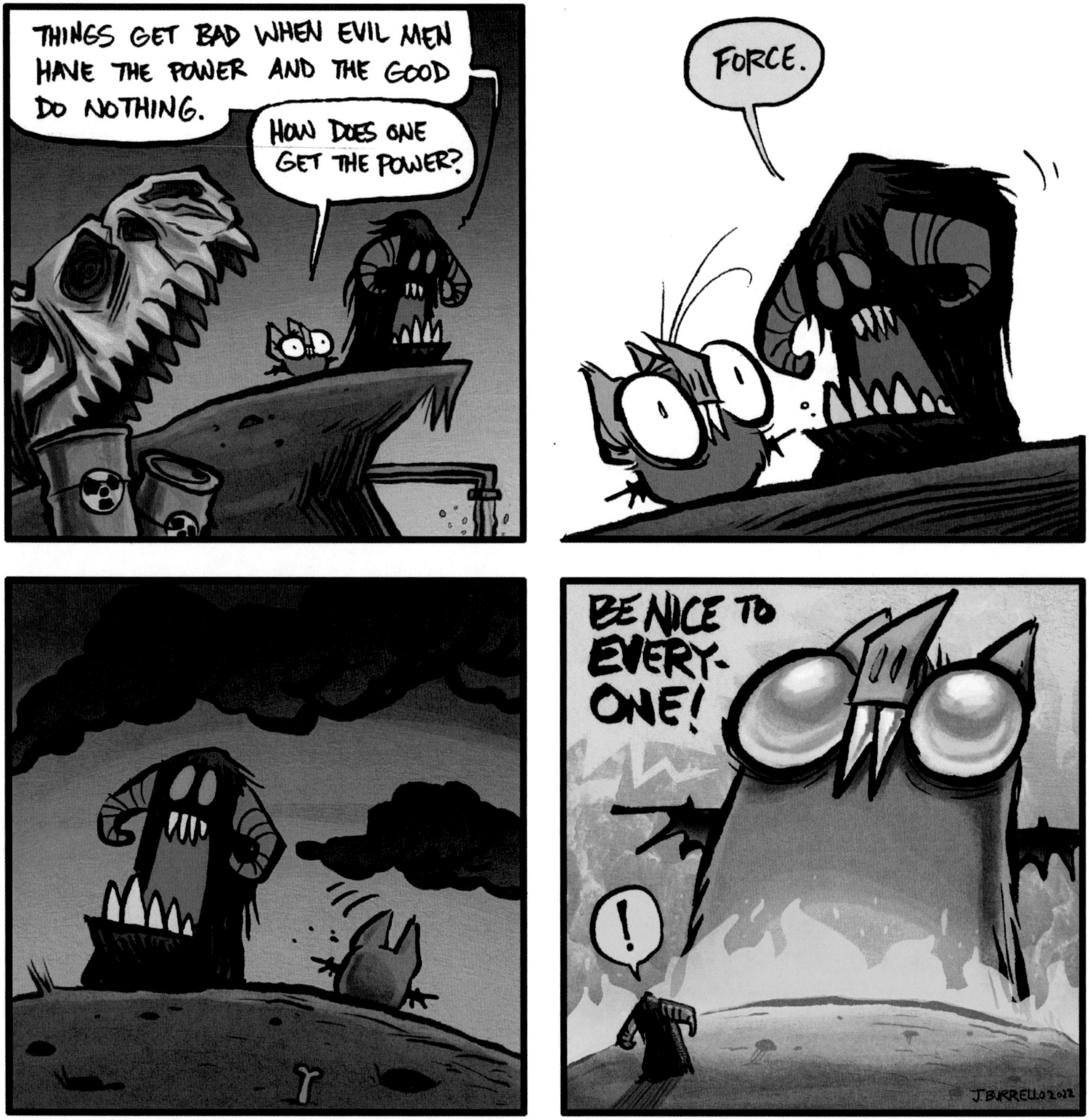
THINGS GET BAD WHEN EVIL MEN HAVE THE POWER AND THE GOOD DO NOTHING.
HOW DOES ONE GET THE POWER?
FORCE.
BE NICE TO EVERY-ONE!
!
J.BURRELL 02022

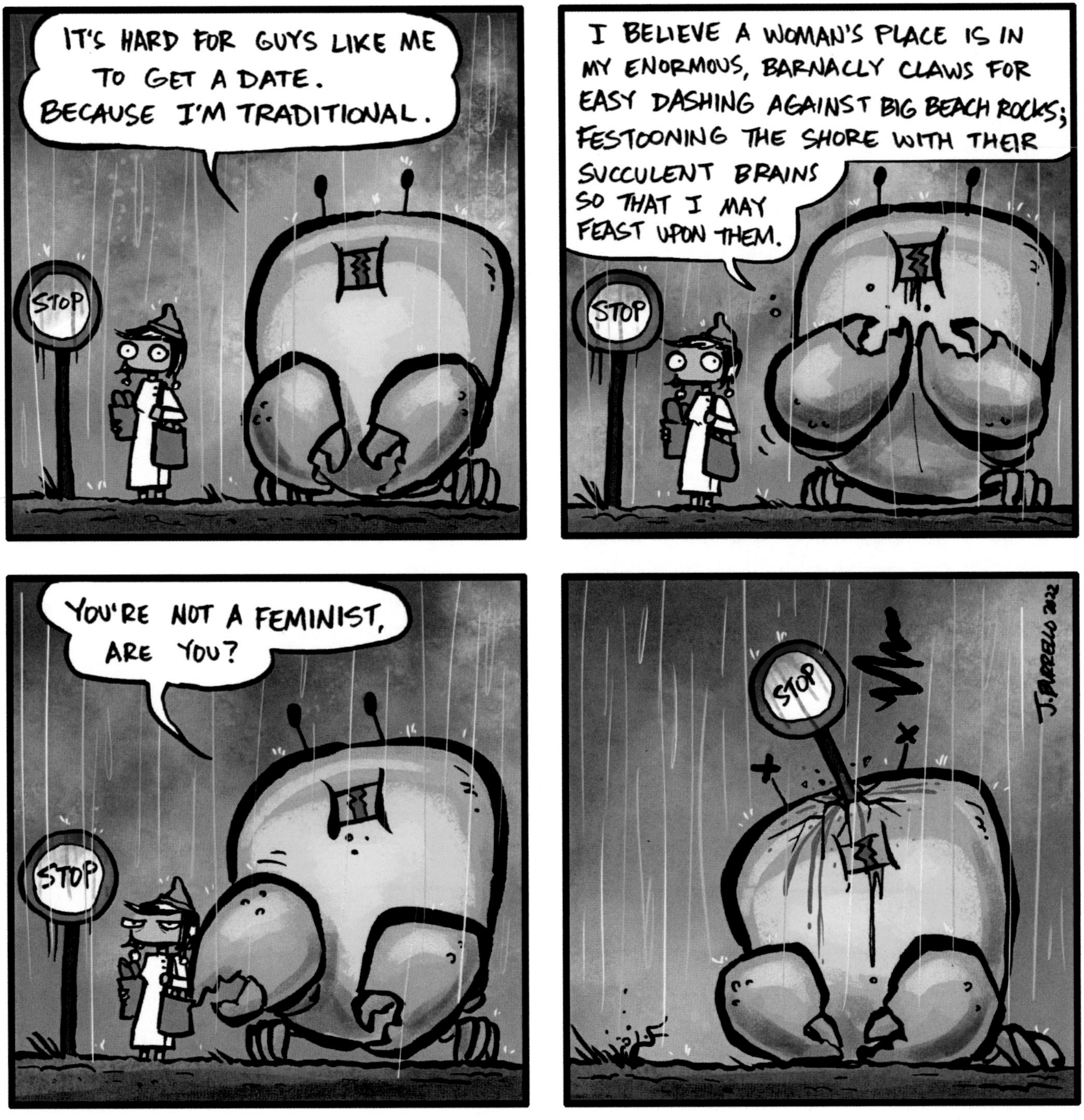
IT'S HARD FOR GUYS LIKE ME TO GET A DATE. BECAUSE I'M TRADITIONAL.
STOP
I BELIEVE A WOMAN'S PLACE IS IN MY ENORMOUS, BARNACLY CLAWS FOR EASY DASHING AGAINST BIG BEACH ROCKS; FESTOONING THE SHORE WITH THEIR SUCCULENT BRAINS SO THAT I MAY FEAST UPON THEM.
STOP
YOU'RE NOT A FEMINIST, ARE YOU?
STOP
J. BARBELLO 2022
STOP

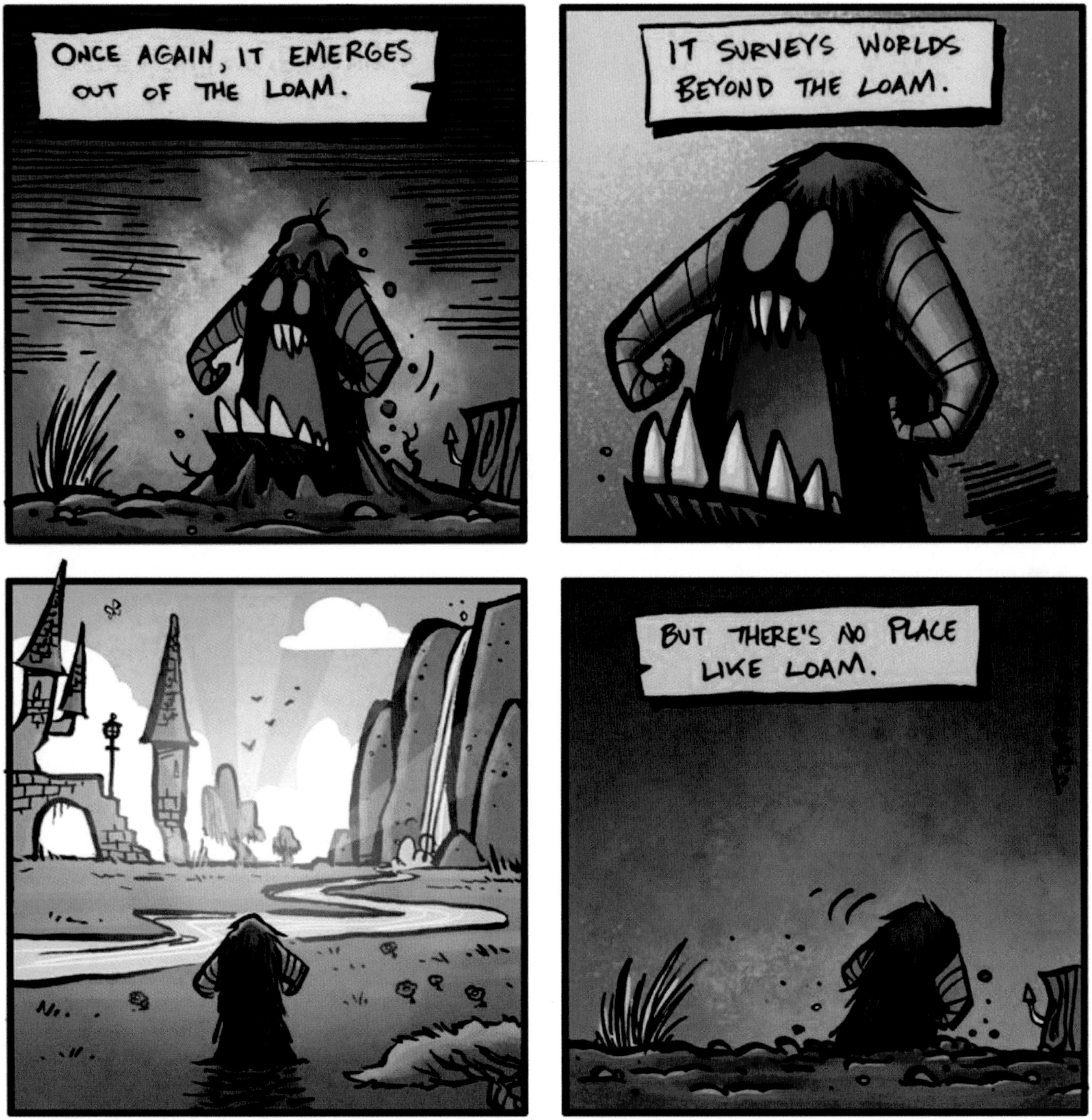
ONCE AGAIN, IT EMERGES OUT OF THE LOAM.
IT SURVEYS WORLDS BEYOND THE LOAM.
BUT THERE'S NO PLACE LIKE LOAM.

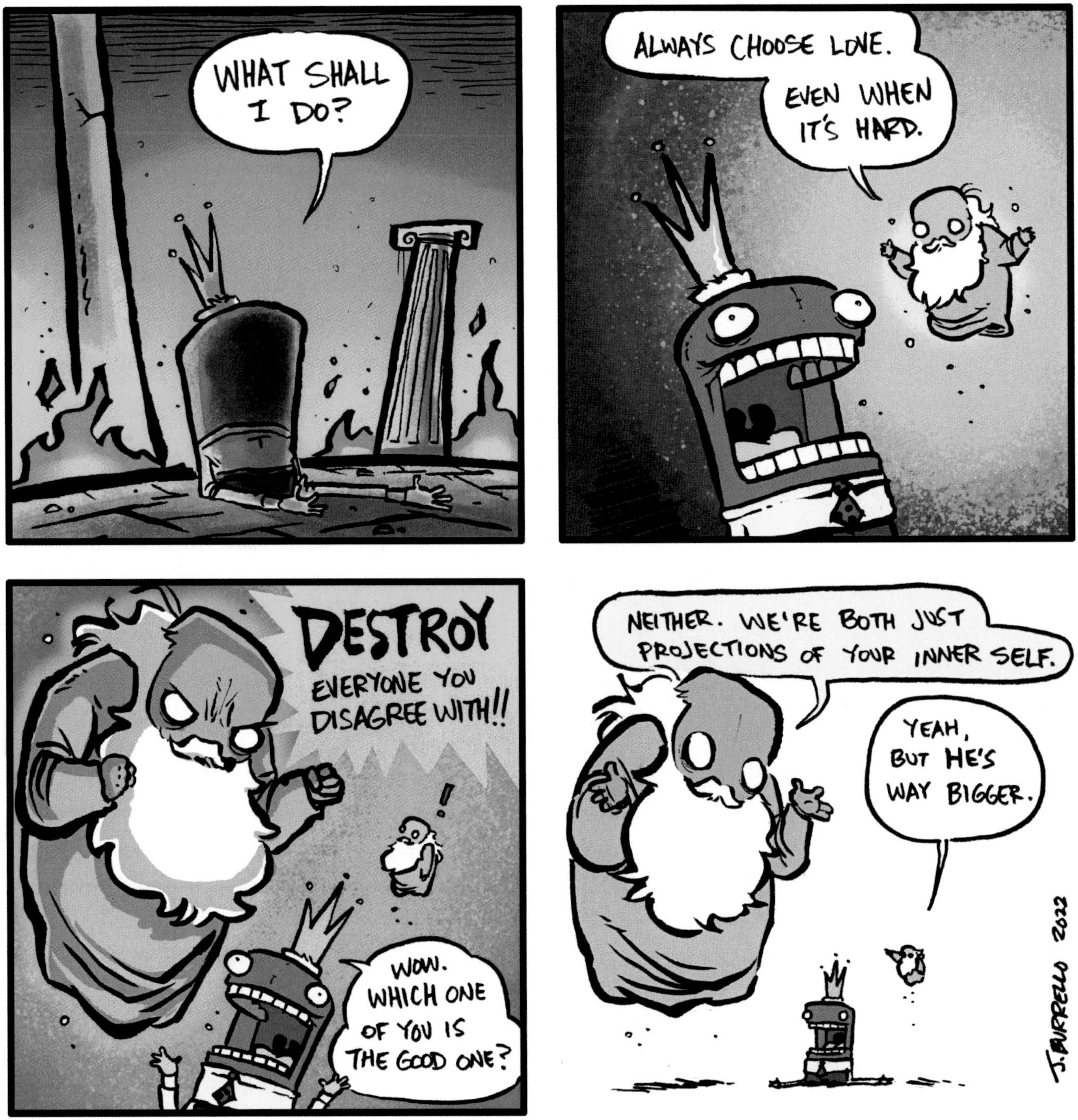
WHAT SHALL I DO?
ALWAYS CHOOSE LOVE.
EVEN WHEN IT'S HARD.
DESTROY EVERYONE YOU DISAGREE WITH!!
!
WOW. WHICH ONE OF YOU IS THE GOOD ONE?
NEITHER. WE'RE BOTH JUST PROJECTIONS OF YOUR INNER SELF.
YEAH, BUT HE'S WAY BIGGER.
J. BURRELLO 2022

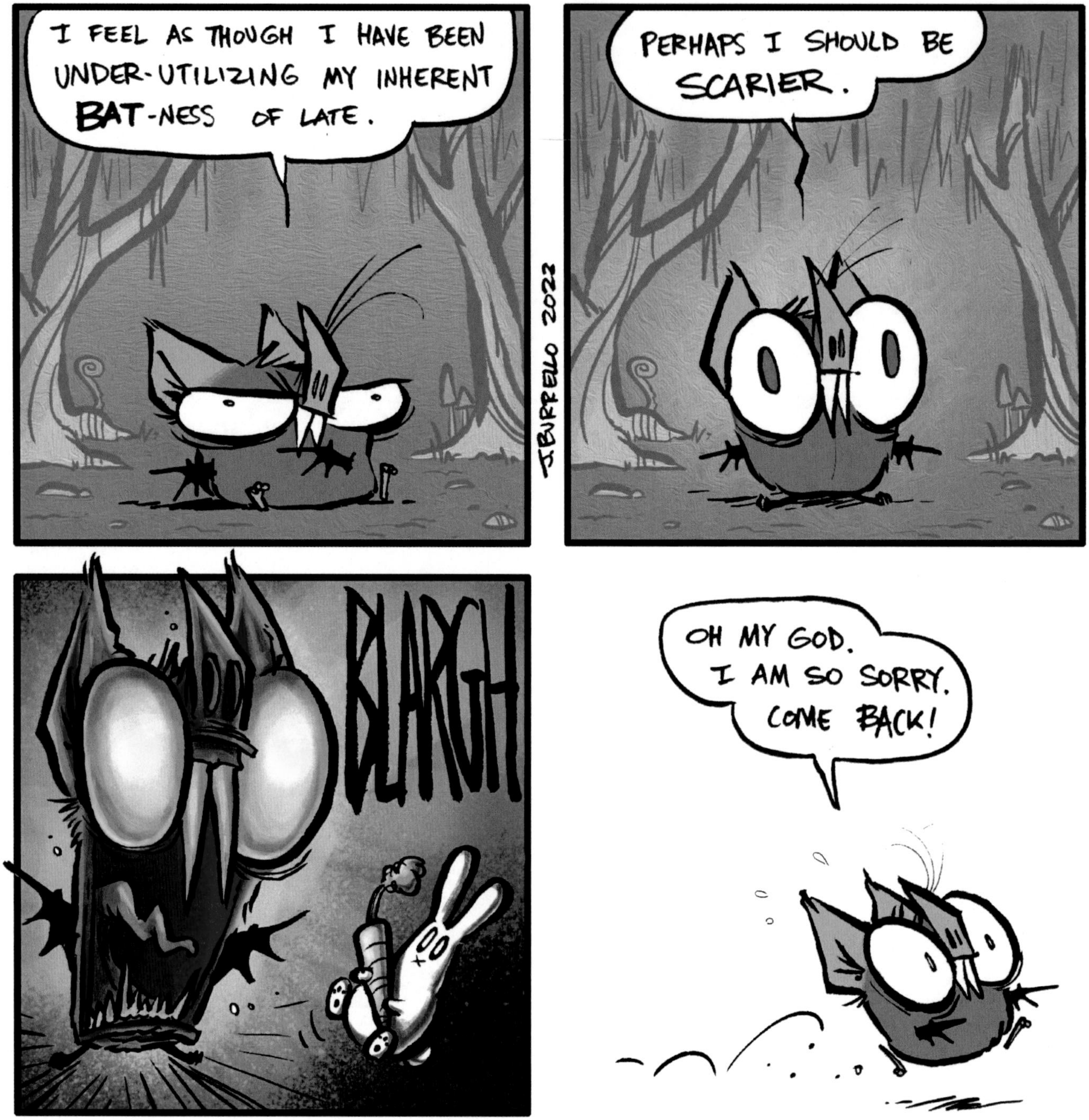
I FEEL AS THOUGH I HAVE BEEN UNDER-UTILIZING MY INHERENT BAT-NESS OF LATE.
J BURRELLO 2022
PERHAPS I SHOULD BE SCARIER.
BLARGH
OH MY GOD. I AM SO SORRY. COME BACK!

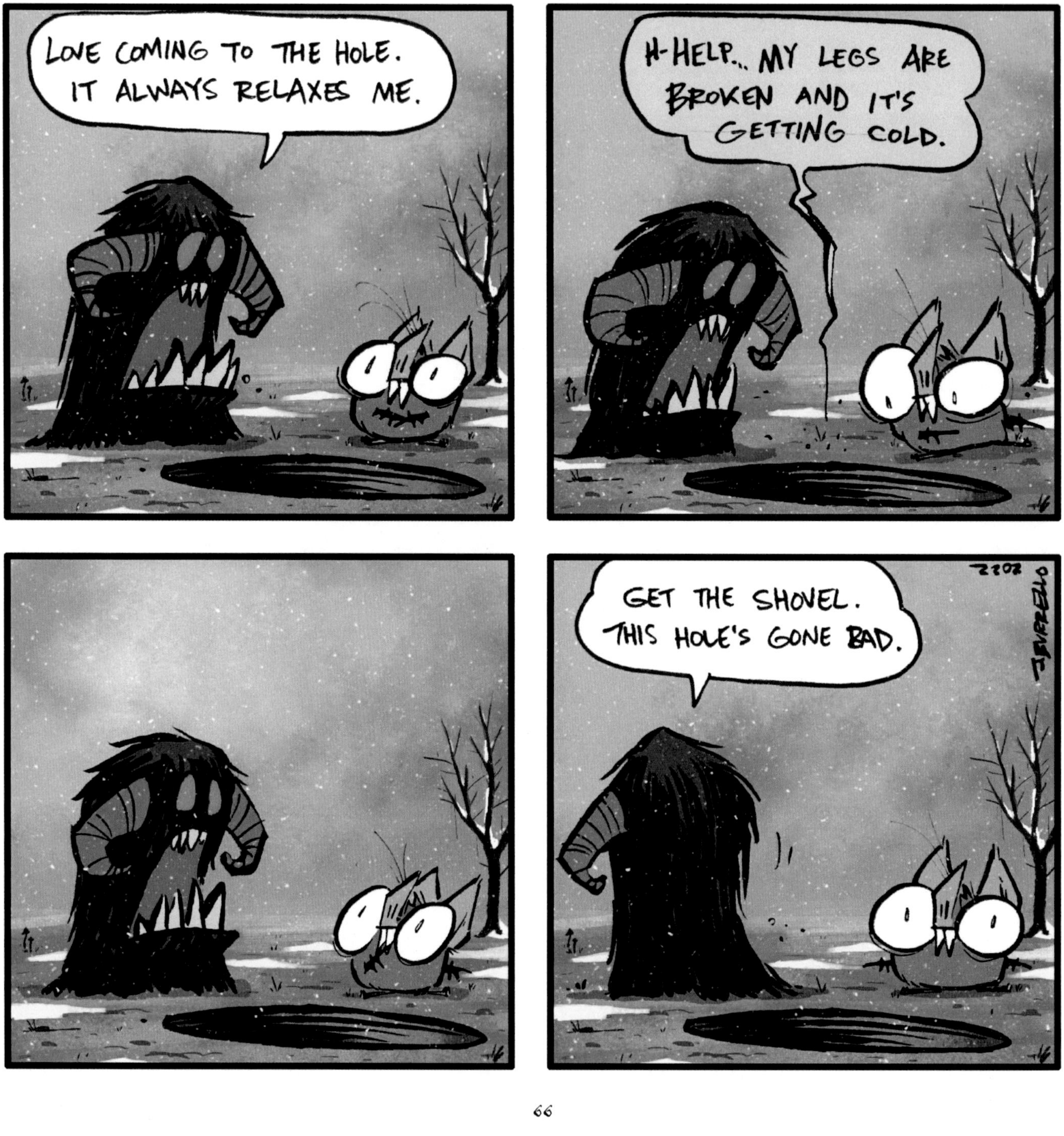
LOVE COMING TO THE HOLE. IT ALWAYS RELAXES ME.
H-HELP... MY LEGS ARE BROKEN AND IT'S GETTING COLD.
GET THE SHOVEL. THIS HOLE'S GONE BAD.

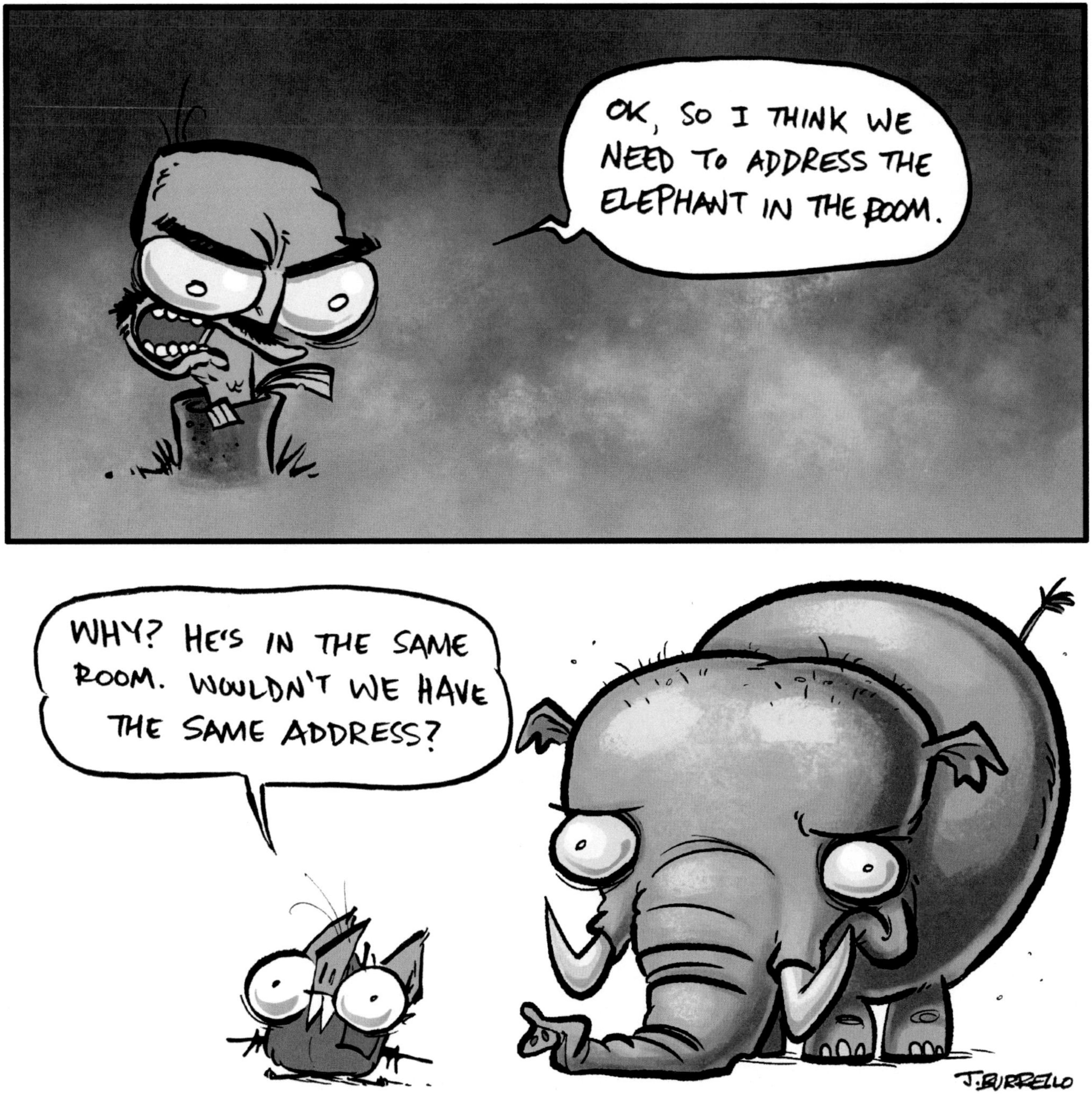
OK, SO I THINK WE NEED TO ADDRESS THE ELEPHANT IN THE ROOM.
WHY? HE'S IN THE SAME ROOM. WOULDN'T WE HAVE THE SAME ADDRESS?
J.BURRELLO

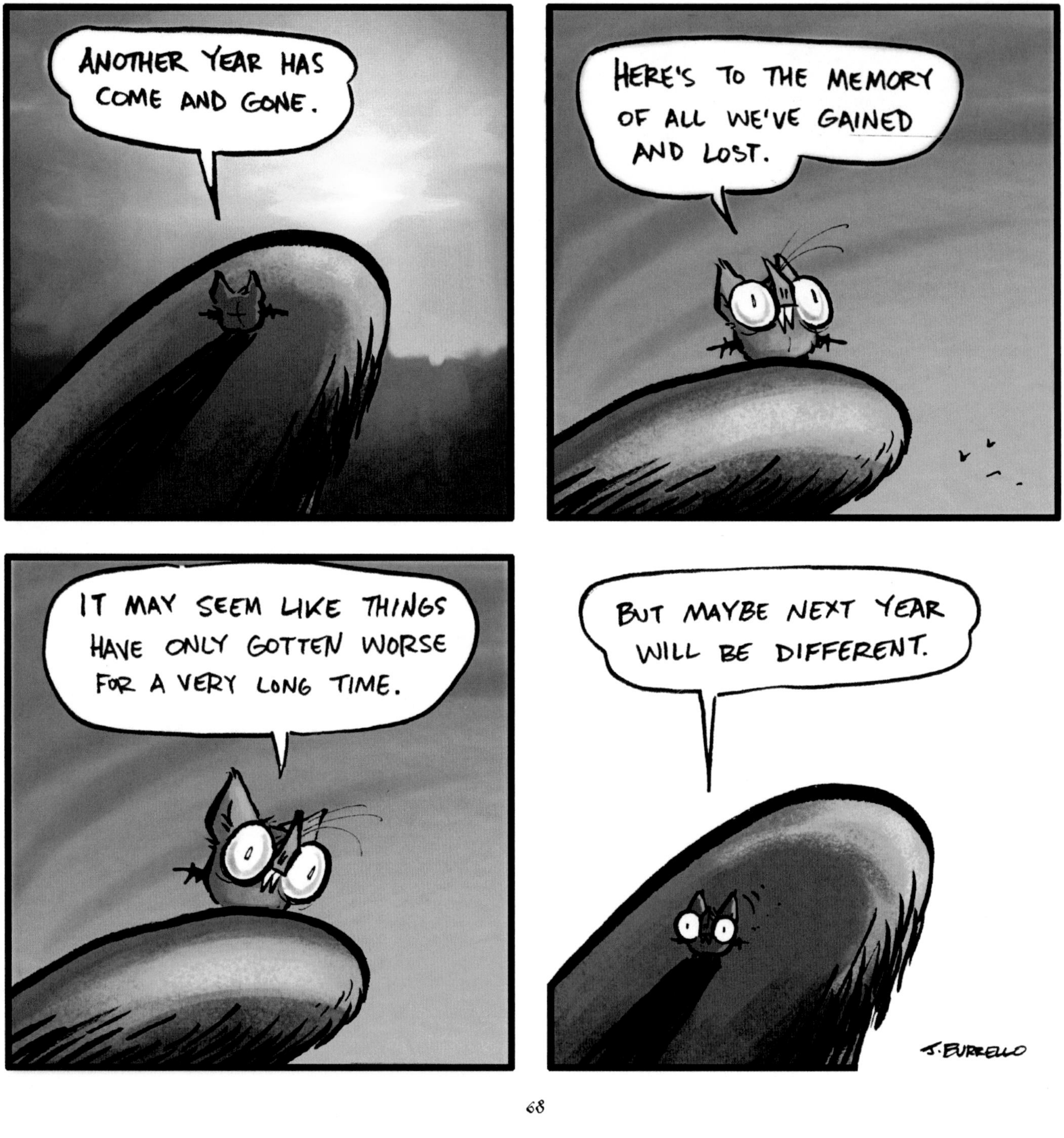
ANOTHER YEAR HAS COME AND GONE.
HERE'S TO THE MEMORY OF ALL WE'VE GAINED AND LOST.
IT MAY SEEM LIKE THINGS HAVE ONLY GOTTEN WORSE FOR A VERY LONG TIME.
BUT MAYBE NEXT YEAR WILL BE DIFFERENT.
J. BURRELLO

LOAM MONSTER

night vision eyes that glow in the dark (super cool)

fuzzy exterior to insulate against the cold, cold loam

hooked horns for digging in the loam

no arms or legs? None needed in the loam

yellow teeth from eating loam

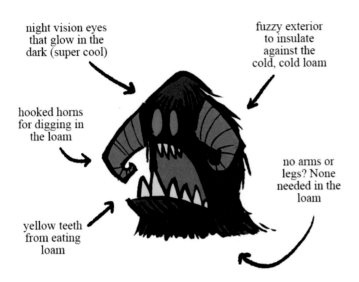

ANTEATER JACK

long snout and sticky tongue for burrowing into couch cushions and eating loose change

poor vision

lost money on crypto and NFTs

$6,000 robe made from endangered porpoise

drinking liquid money??

driven by profit

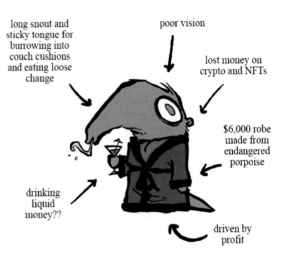

RABBIT

the most mysterious creature in the known universe

ears?? what are these? could they be for murder??

carrot

it's desires: unknown

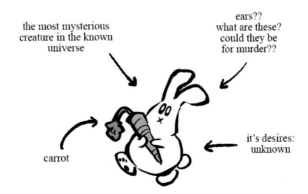

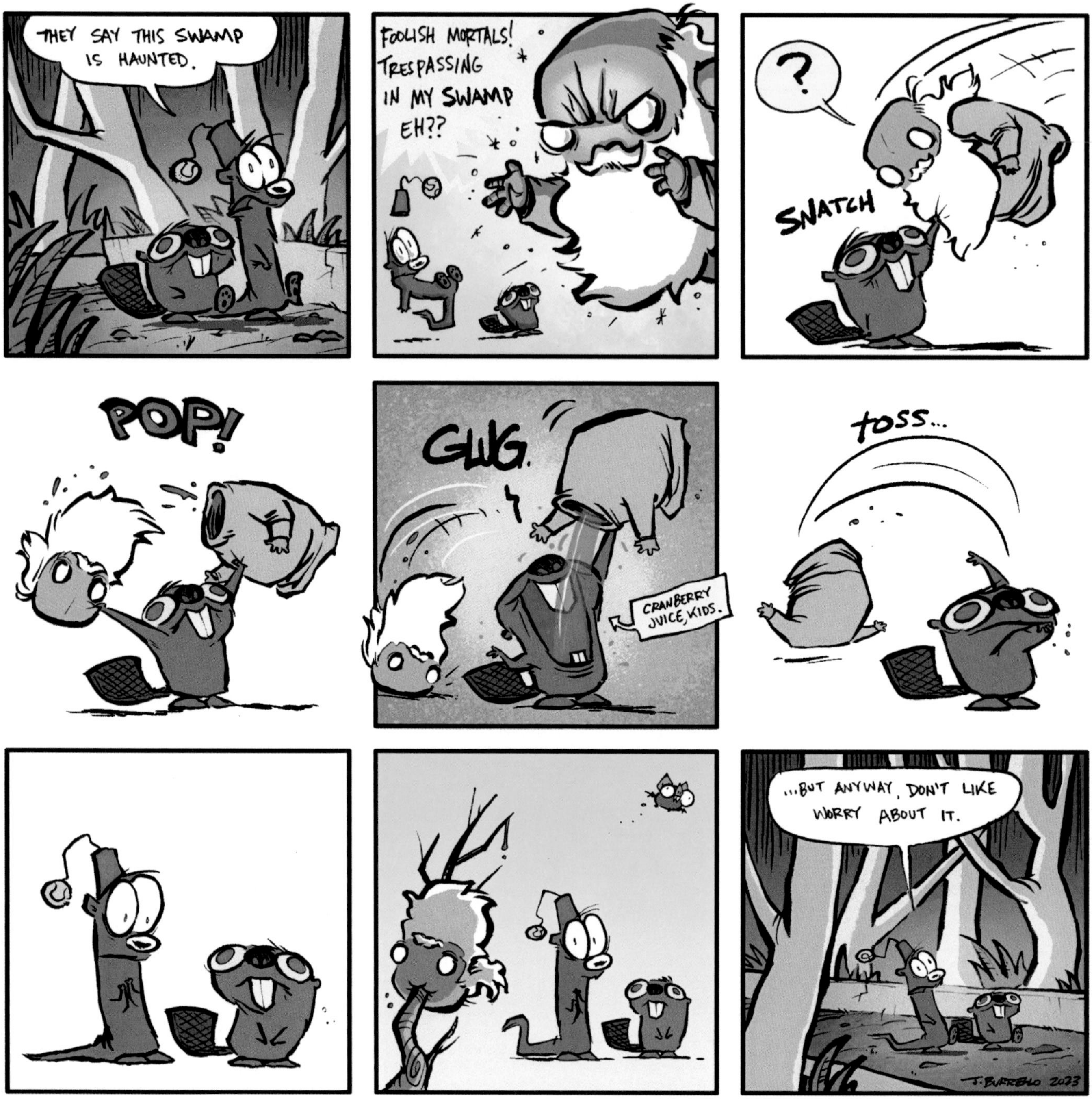
THEY SAY THIS SWAMP IS HAUNTED.
FOOLISH MORTALS! TRESPASSING IN MY SWAMP EH??
?
SNATCH
POP!
GUG.
CRANBERRY JUICE, KIDS.
toss...
...BUT ANYWAY, DON'T LIKE WORRY ABOUT IT.
J. BURRELLO 2023

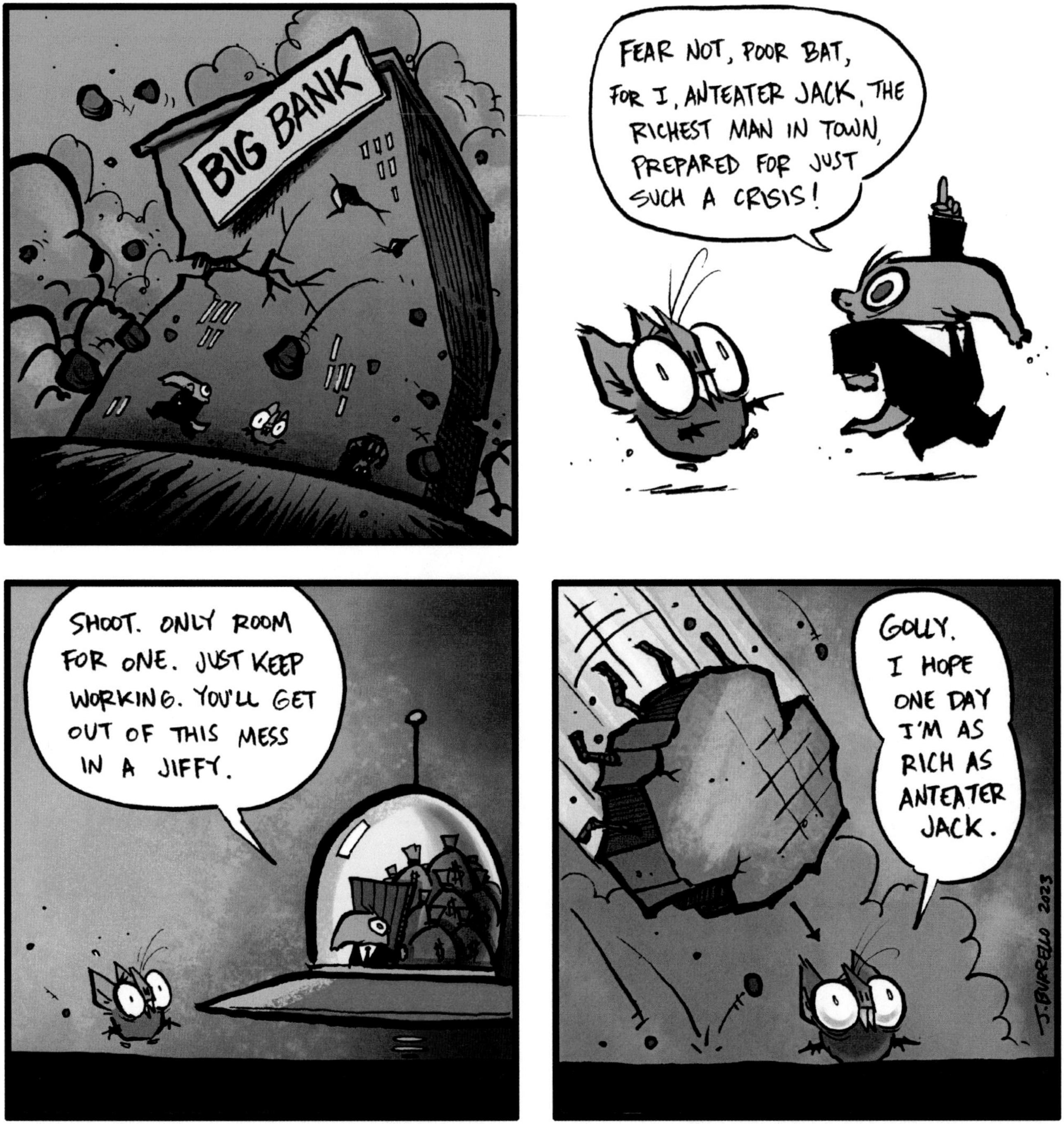
BIG BANK
FEAR NOT, POOR BAT, FOR I, ANTEATER JACK, THE RICHEST MAN IN TOWN, PREPARED FOR JUST SUCH A CRISIS!
SHOOT. ONLY ROOM FOR ONE. JUST KEEP WORKING. YOU'LL GET OUT OF THIS MESS IN A JIFFY.
GOLLY. I HOPE ONE DAY I'M AS RICH AS ANTEATER JACK.
J. BURRELLO 2023

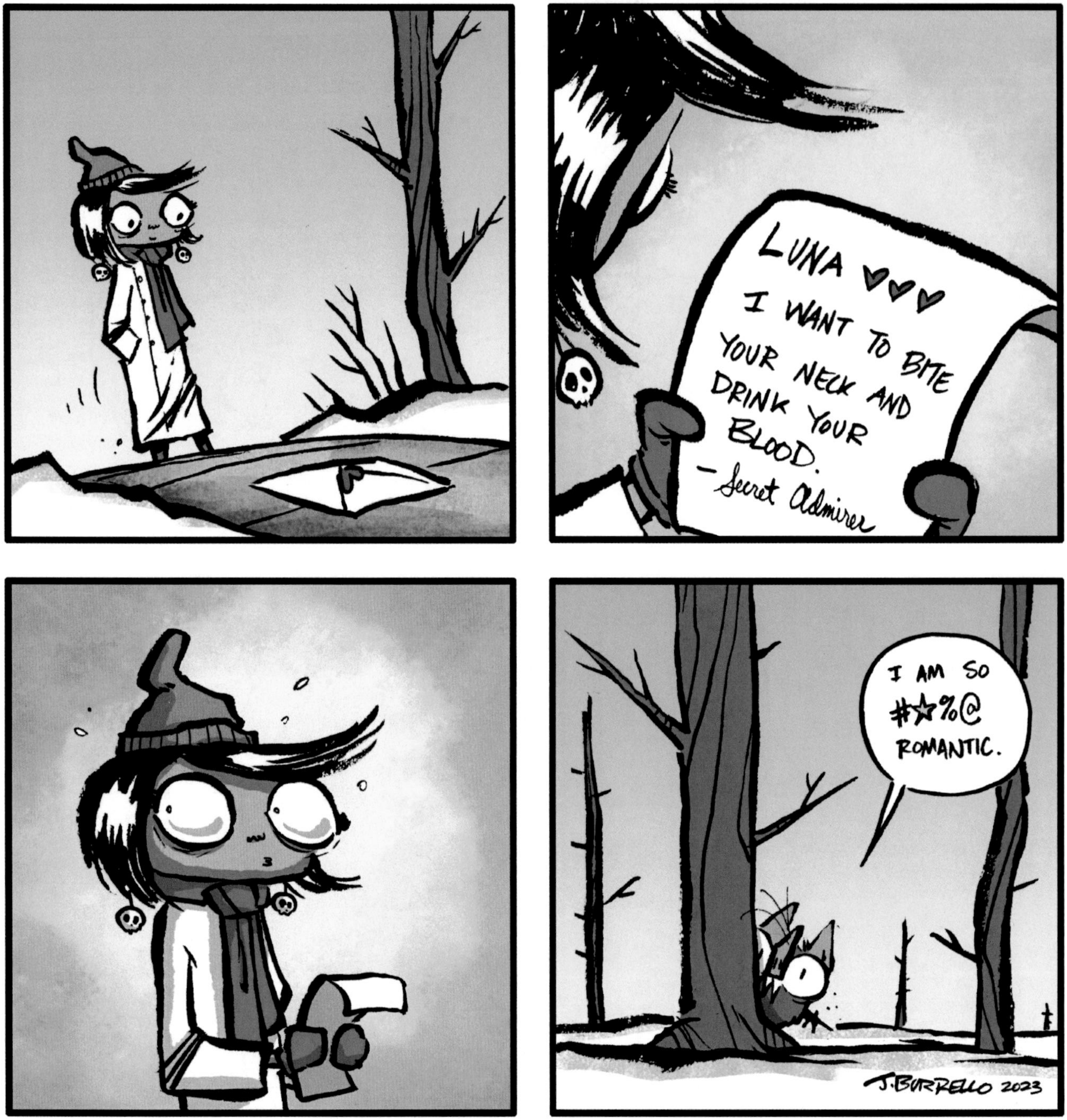
LUNA ♥♥♥
I WANT TO BITE YOUR NECK AND DRINK YOUR BLOOD.
—Secret Admirer
I AM SO #☆%@ ROMANTIC.
J.BURRELLO 2023

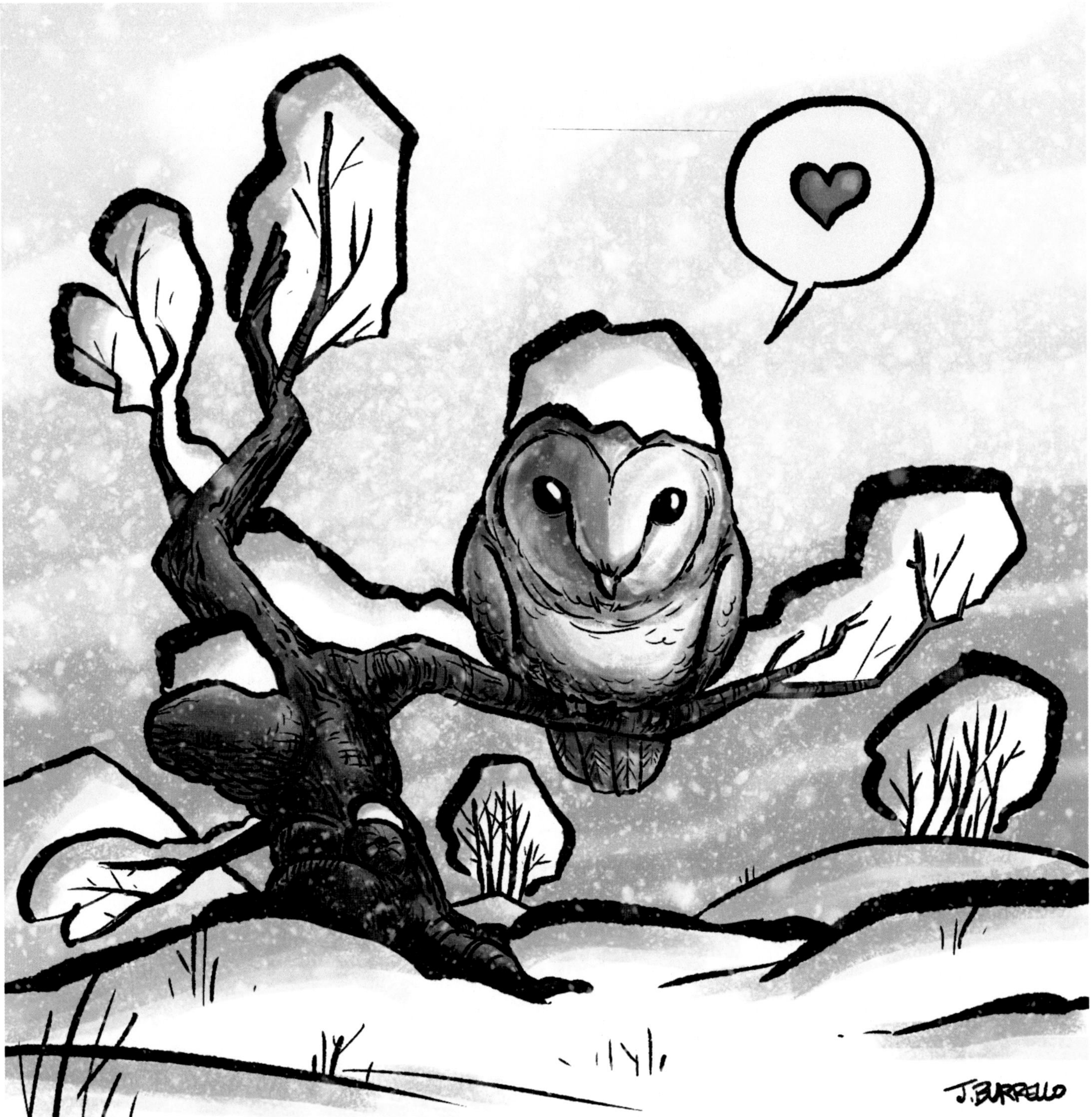
J.BURRELLO

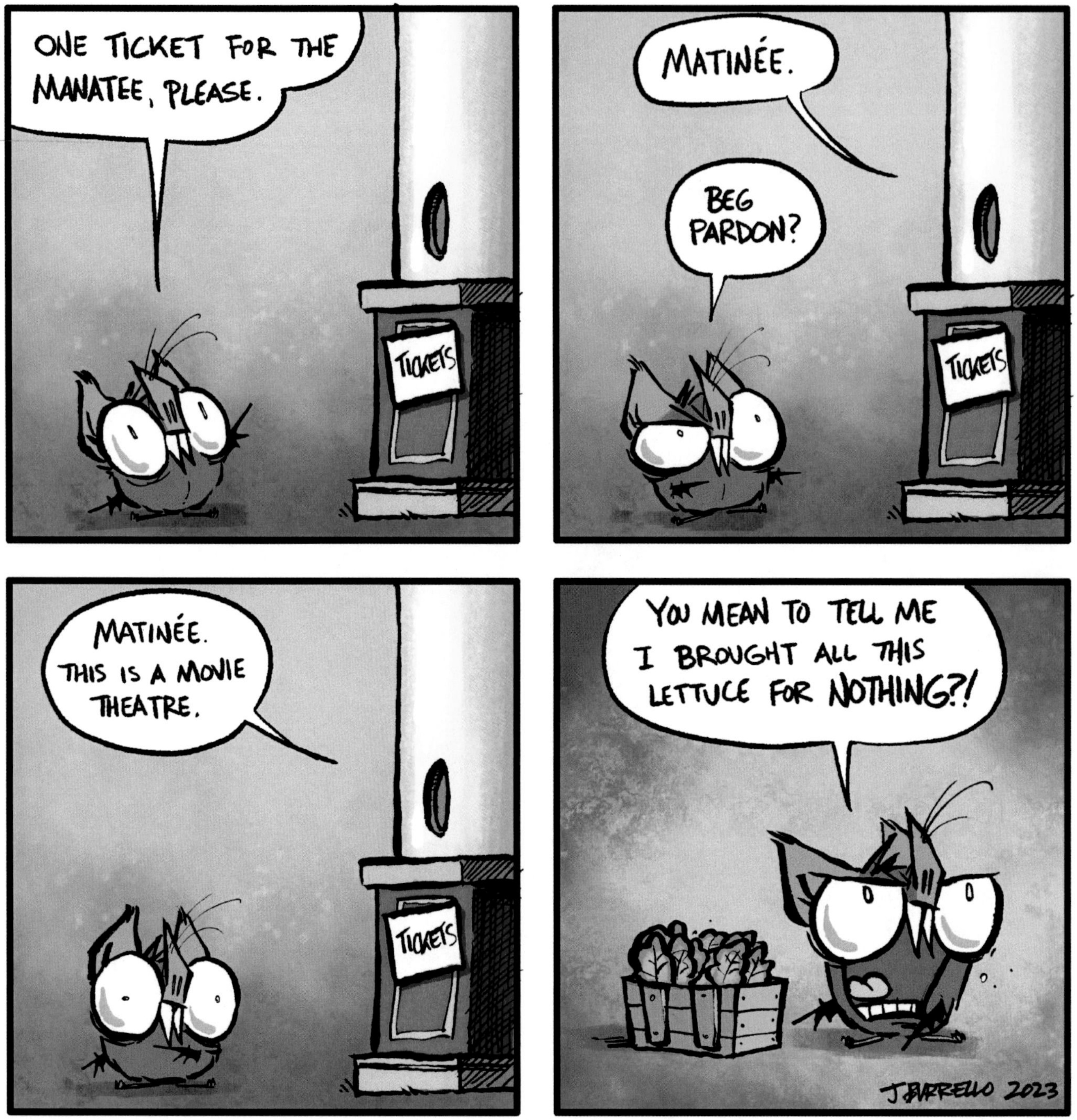
ONE TICKET FOR THE MANATEE, PLEASE.
TICKETS
MATINÉE.
BEG PARDON?
TICKETS
MATINÉE. THIS IS A MOVIE THEATRE.
TICKETS
YOU MEAN TO TELL ME I BROUGHT ALL THIS LETTUCE FOR NOTHING?!
J BURRELLO 2023

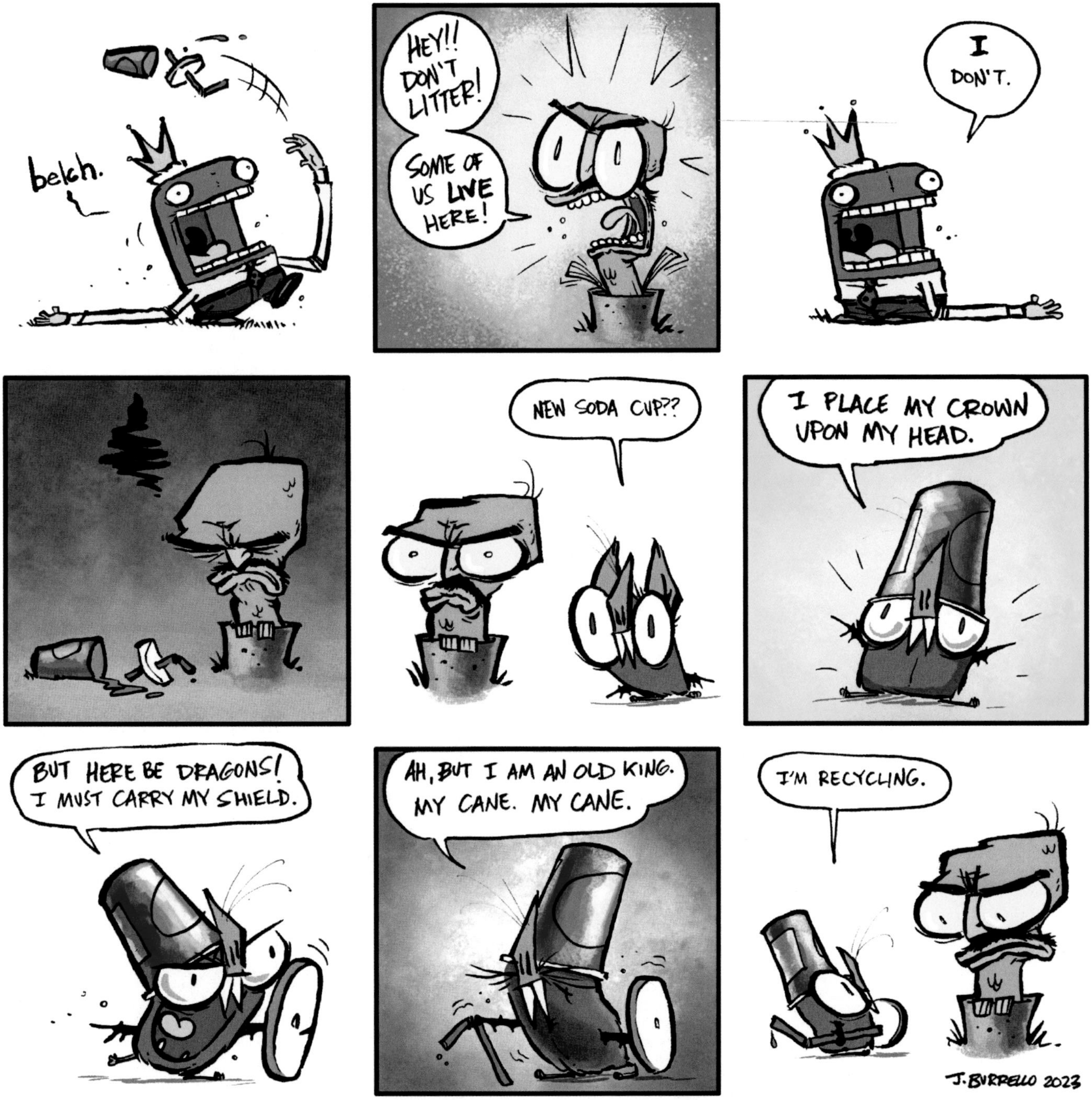
belch.
HEY!! DON'T LITTER!
SOME OF US LIVE HERE!
I DON'T.
NEW SODA CUP??
I PLACE MY CROWN UPON MY HEAD.
BUT HERE BE DRAGONS! I MUST CARRY MY SHIELD.
AH, BUT I AM AN OLD KING. MY CANE. MY CANE.
I'M RECYCLING.
J. BURRELLO 2023

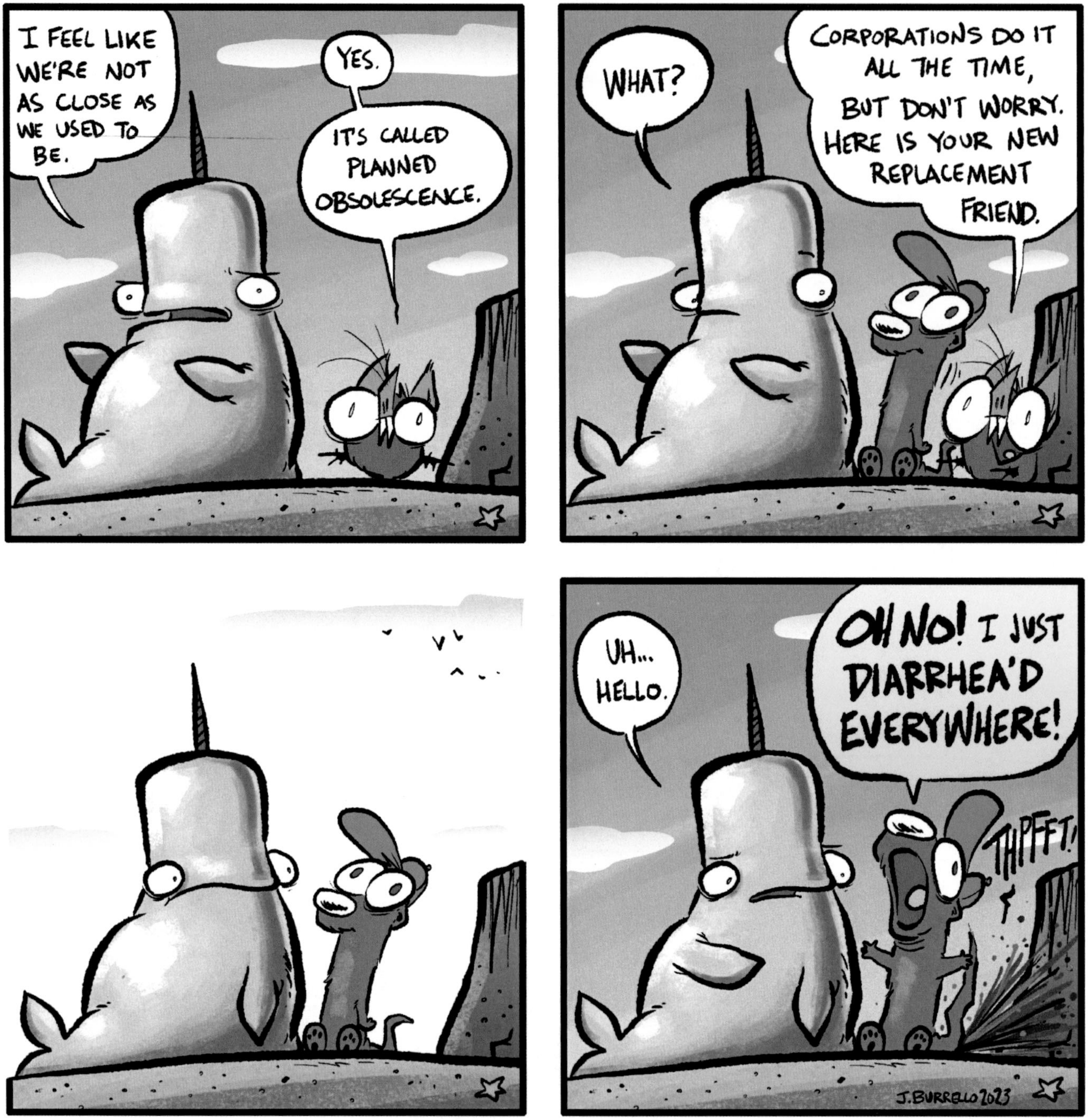
I FEEL LIKE WE'RE NOT AS CLOSE AS WE USED TO BE.
YES.
IT'S CALLED PLANNED OBSOLESCENCE.
WHAT?
CORPORATIONS DO IT ALL THE TIME,
BUT DON'T WORRY. HERE IS YOUR NEW REPLACEMENT FRIEND.
UH... HELLO.
OH NO! I JUST DIARRHEA'D EVERYWHERE!
THPFFT!
J.BURRELLO 2023

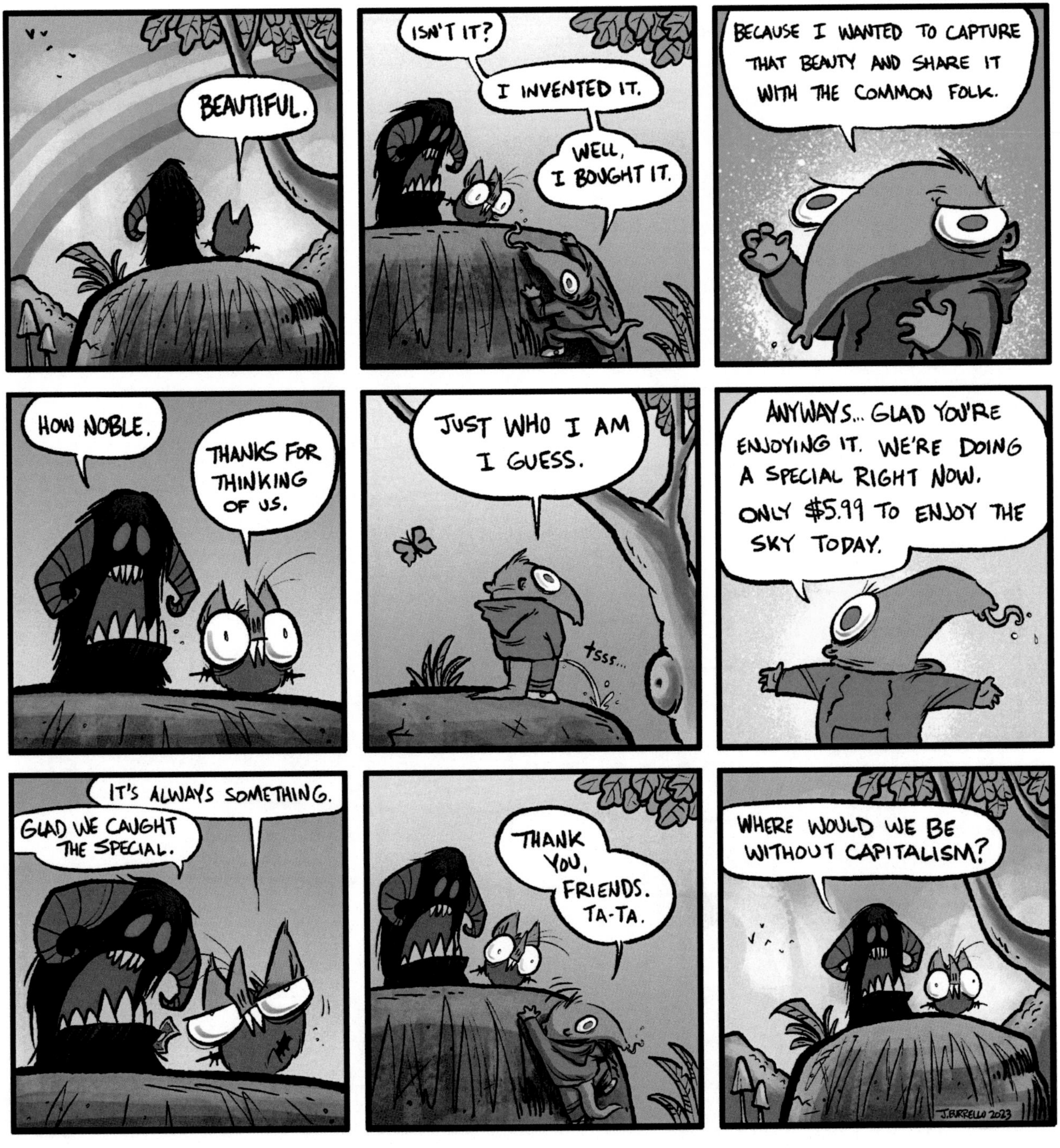
BEAUTIFUL.
ISN'T IT?
I INVENTED IT.
WELL, I BOUGHT IT.
BECAUSE I WANTED TO CAPTURE THAT BEAUTY AND SHARE IT WITH THE COMMON FOLK.
HOW NOBLE.
THANKS FOR THINKING OF US.
JUST WHO I AM I GUESS.
tsss...
ANYWAYS... GLAD YOU'RE ENJOYING IT. WE'RE DOING A SPECIAL RIGHT NOW. ONLY $5.99 TO ENJOY THE SKY TODAY.
GLAD WE CAUGHT THE SPECIAL.
IT'S ALWAYS SOMETHING.
THANK YOU, FRIENDS. TA-TA.
WHERE WOULD WE BE WITHOUT CAPITALISM?
J.BURRELLO 2023

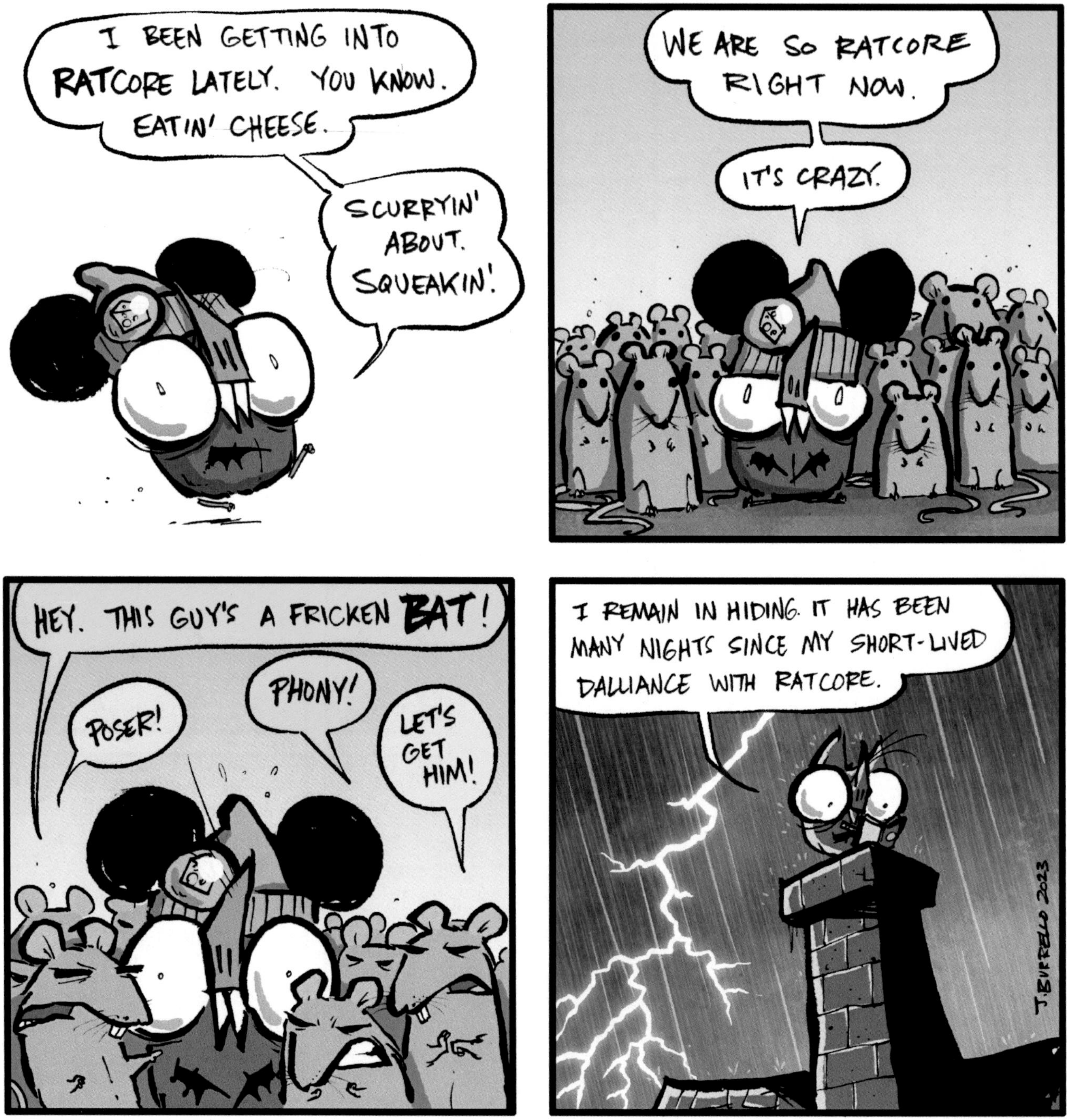
I BEEN GETTING INTO RATCORE LATELY. YOU KNOW. EATIN' CHEESE.
SCURRYIN' ABOUT. SQUEAKIN'!
WE ARE SO RATCORE RIGHT NOW.
IT'S CRAZY.
HEY. THIS GUY'S A FRICKEN BAT!
POSER!
PHONY!
LET'S GET HIM!
I REMAIN IN HIDING. IT HAS BEEN MANY NIGHTS SINCE MY SHORT-LIVED DALLIANCE WITH RATCORE.
J. BURRELLO 2023

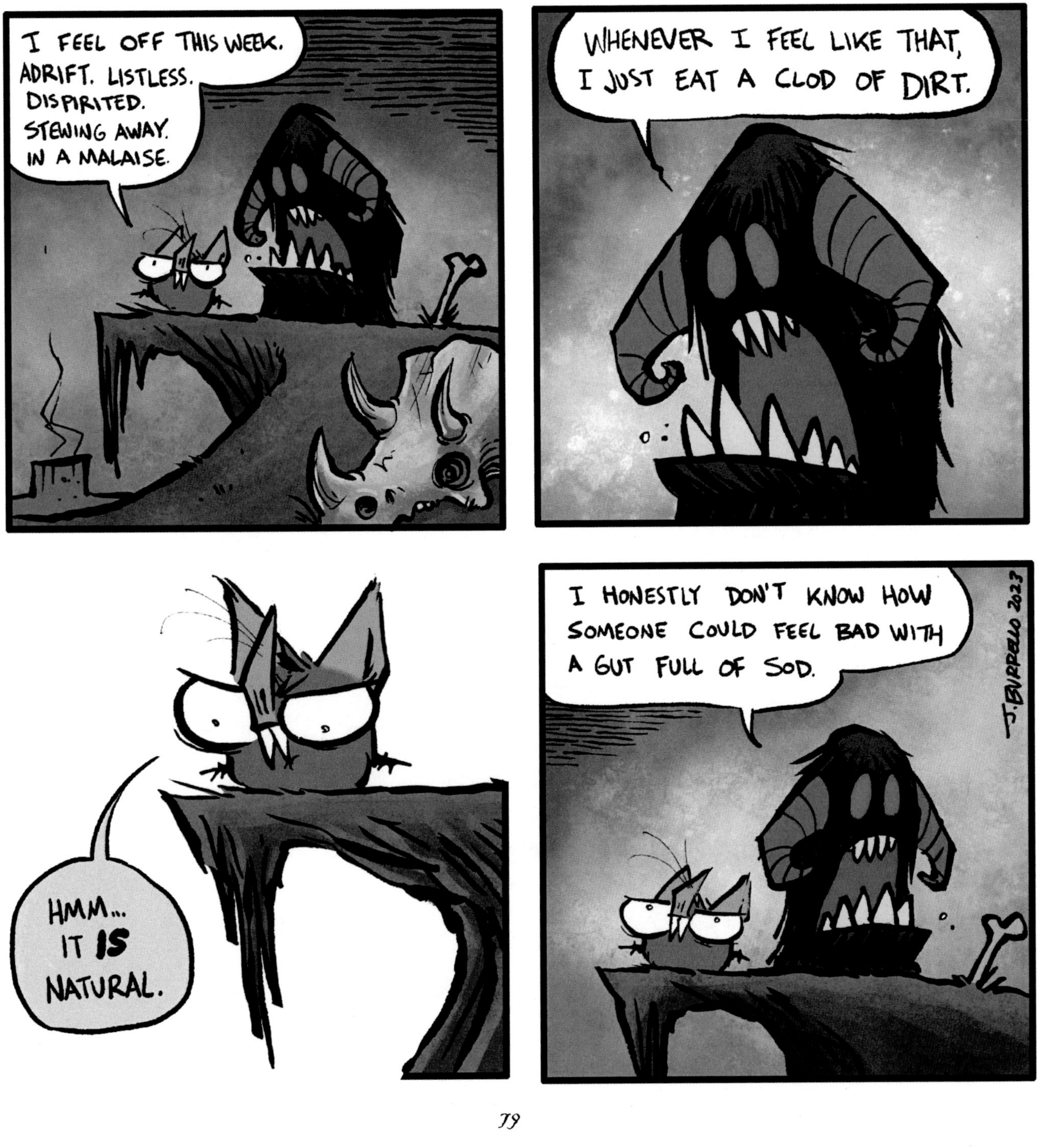
I FEEL OFF THIS WEEK. ADRIFT. LISTLESS. DISPIRITED. STEWING AWAY. IN A MALAISE.
WHENEVER I FEEL LIKE THAT, I JUST EAT A CLOD OF DIRT.
HMM... IT **IS** NATURAL.
I HONESTLY DON'T KNOW HOW SOMEONE COULD FEEL BAD WITH A GUT FULL OF SOD.
J. BURRELLO 2023

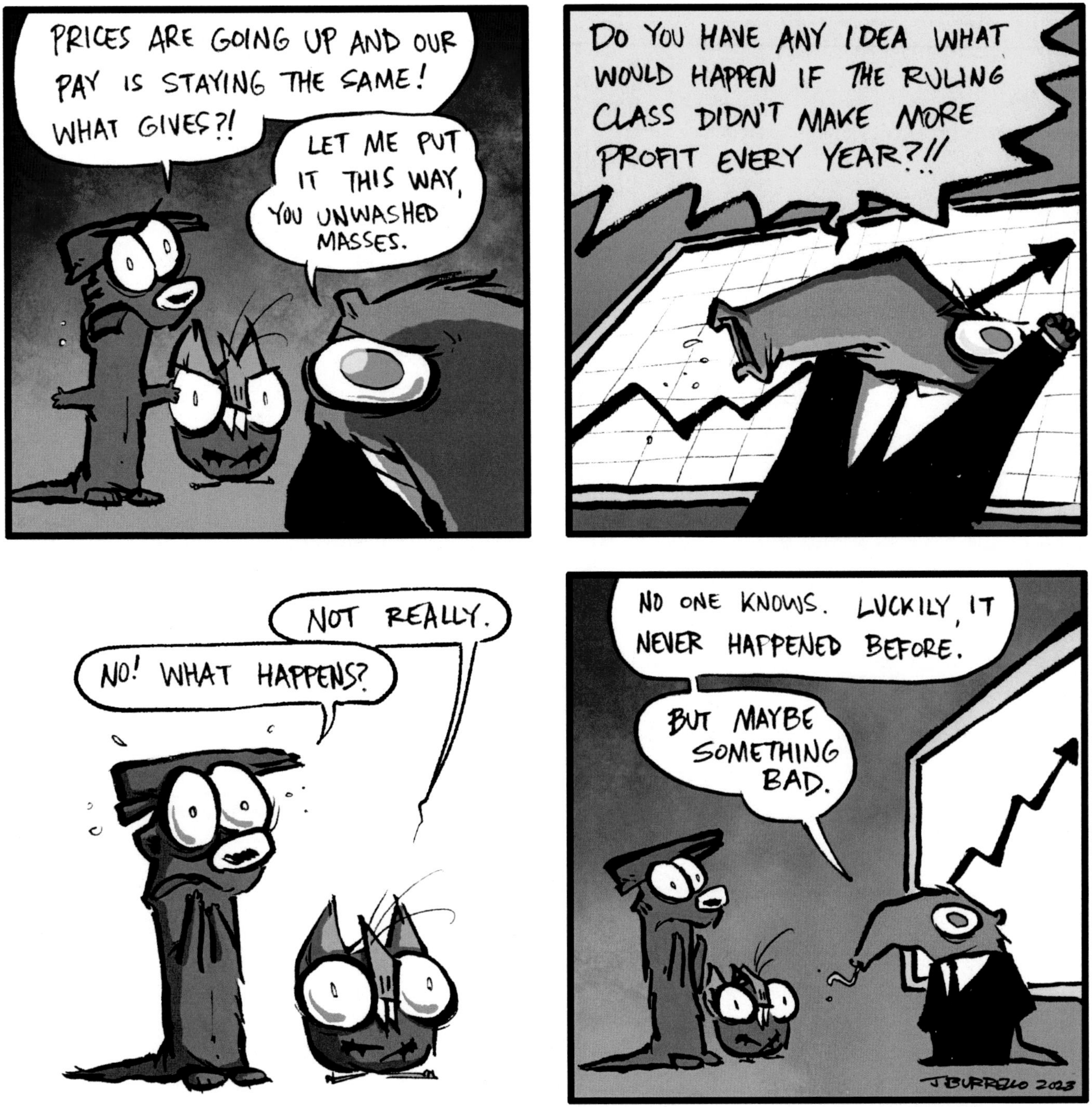
PRICES ARE GOING UP AND OUR PAY IS STAYING THE SAME! WHAT GIVES?!
LET ME PUT IT THIS WAY, YOU UNWASHED MASSES.
DO YOU HAVE ANY IDEA WHAT WOULD HAPPEN IF THE RULING CLASS DIDN'T MAKE MORE PROFIT EVERY YEAR?!!
NO! WHAT HAPPENS?
NOT REALLY.
NO ONE KNOWS. LUCKILY, IT NEVER HAPPENED BEFORE.
BUT MAYBE SOMETHING BAD.
J BURRELLO 2023

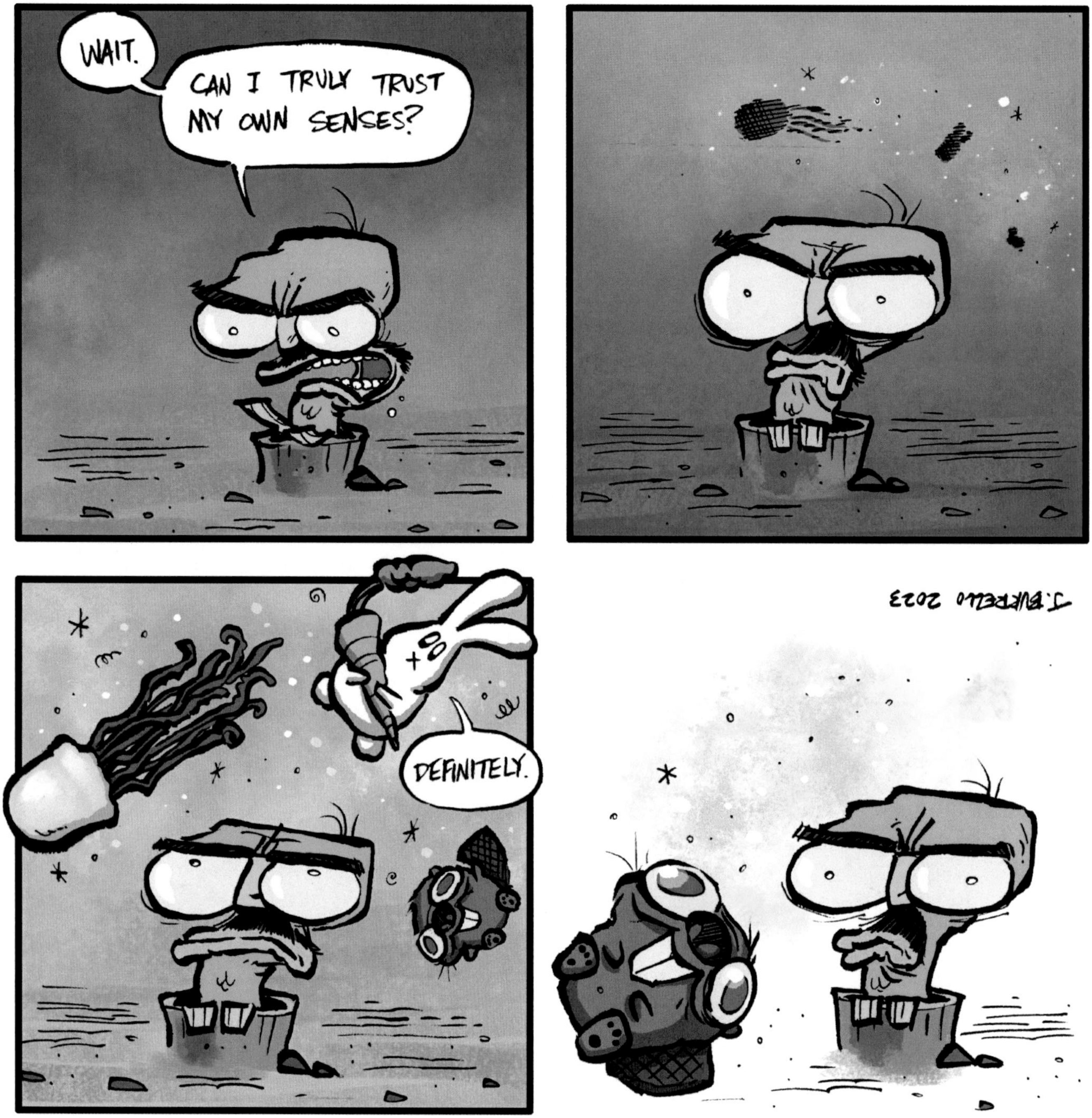
WAIT.
CAN I TRULY TRUST MY OWN SENSES?
DEFINITELY.
J. BURRELLO 2023

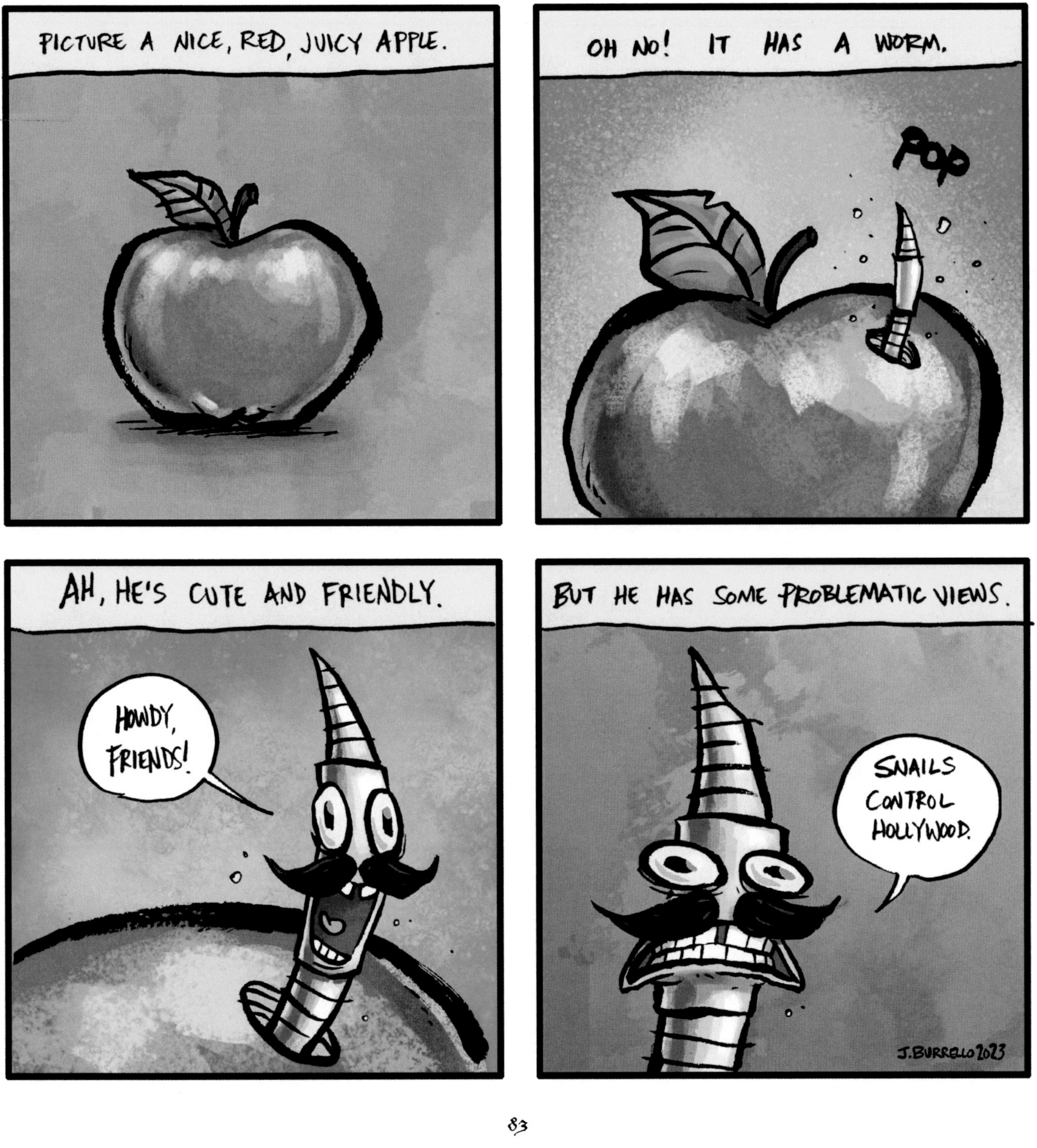
PICTURE A NICE, RED, JUICY APPLE.
OH NO! IT HAS A WORM.
POP
AH, HE'S CUTE AND FRIENDLY.
HOWDY, FRIENDS!
BUT HE HAS SOME PROBLEMATIC VIEWS.
SNAILS CONTROL HOLLYWOOD.
J.BURRELLO 2023

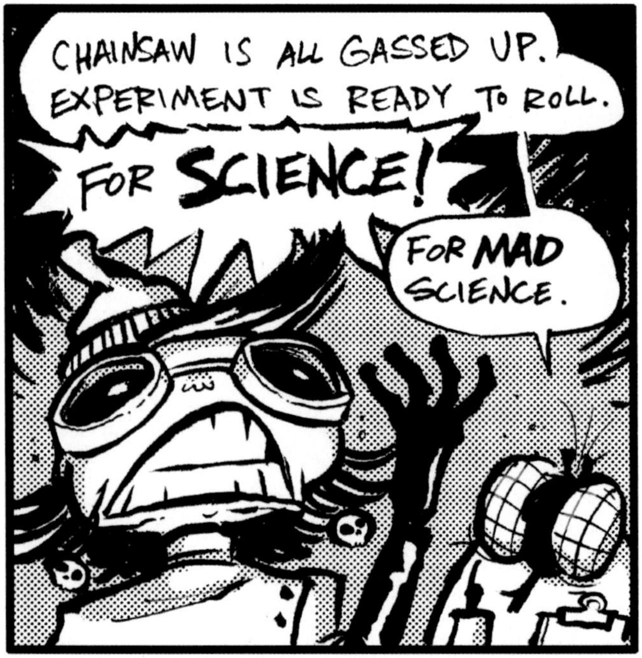
CHAINSAW IS ALL GASSED UP.
EXPERIMENT IS READY TO ROLL.
FOR SCIENCE!
FOR MAD SCIENCE.

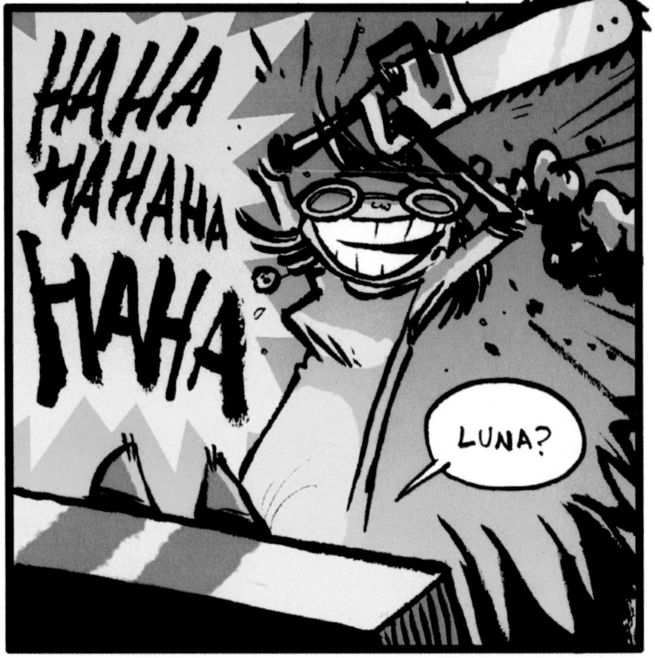
HAHA HAHAHA HAHA
LUNA?

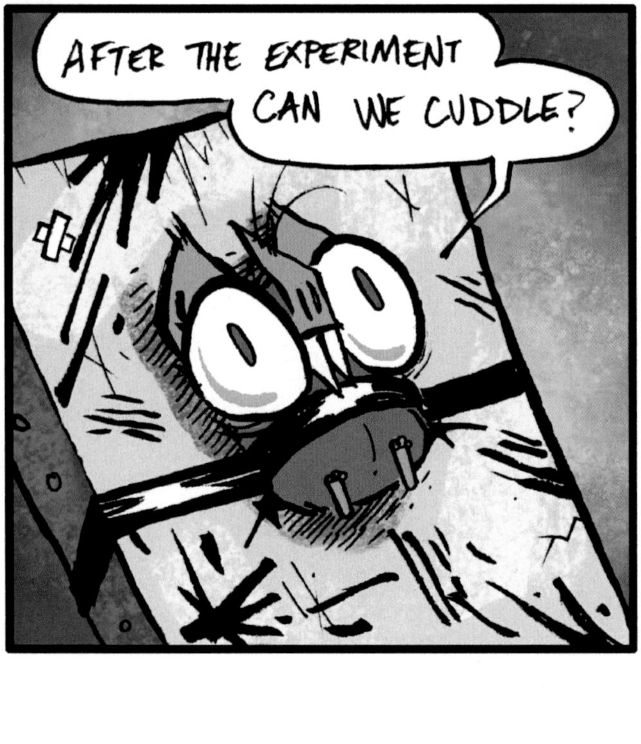
AFTER THE EXPERIMENT CAN WE CUDDLE?

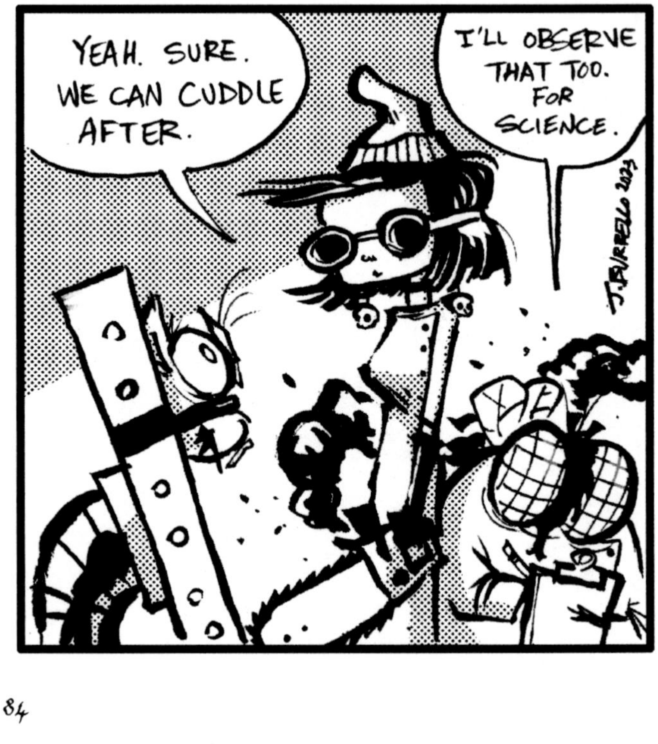
YEAH. SURE. WE CAN CUDDLE AFTER.
I'LL OBSERVE THAT TOO. FOR SCIENCE.
J.BURRELLO 2023

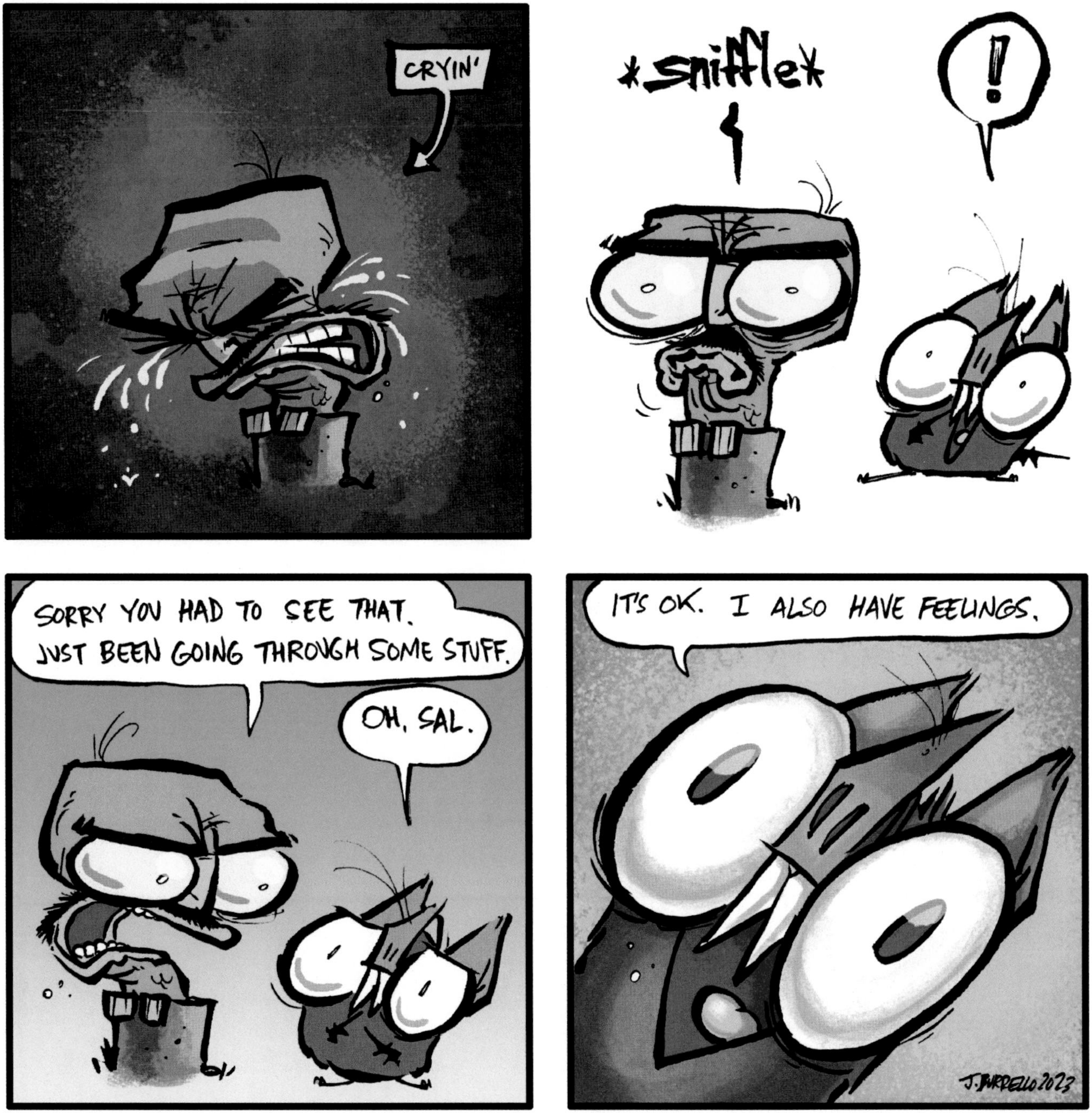
CRYIN'
sniffle
!
SORRY YOU HAD TO SEE THAT. JUST BEEN GOING THROUGH SOME STUFF.
OH, SAL.
IT'S OK. I ALSO HAVE FEELINGS.
J.BURRELLO 2023

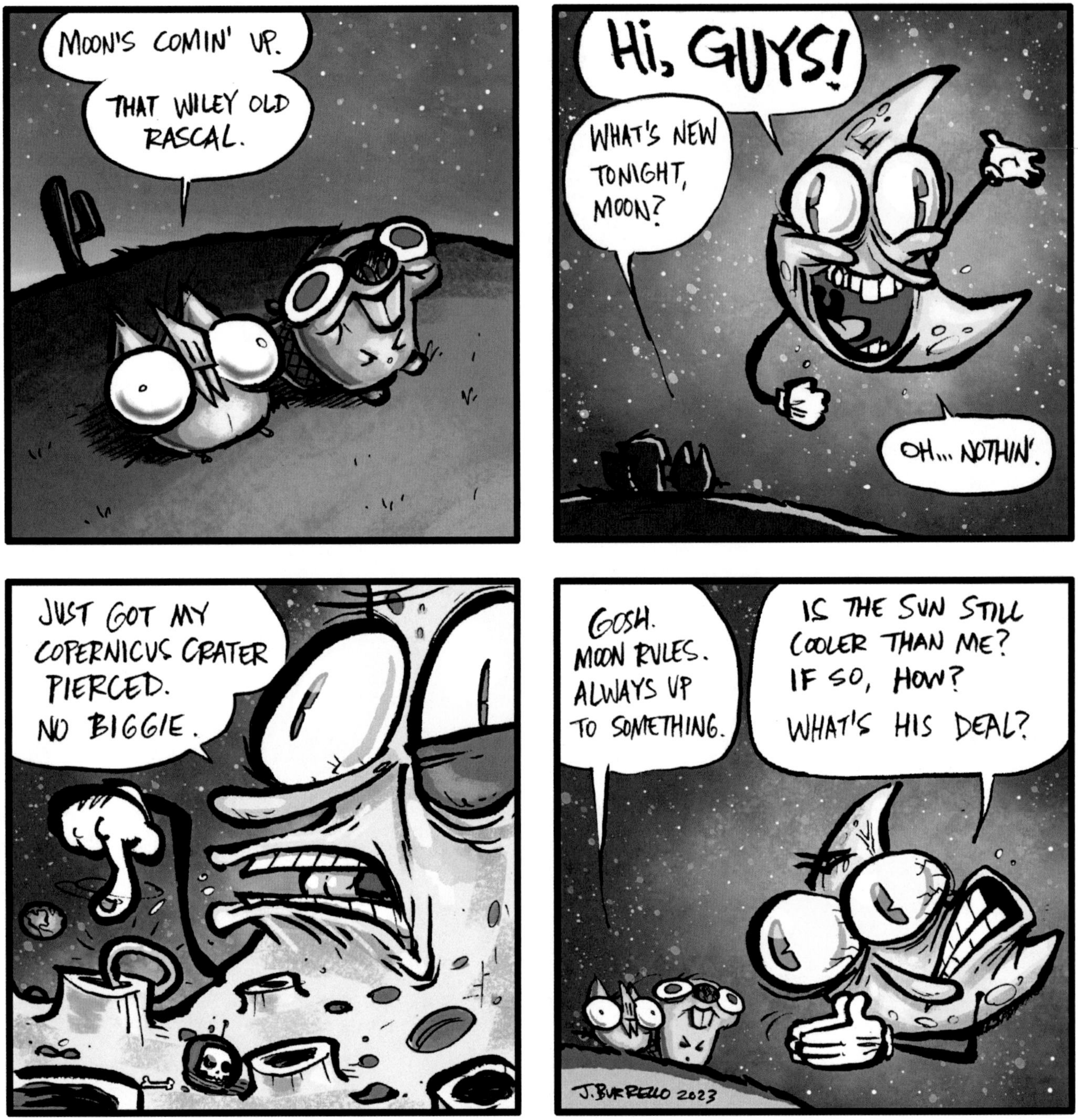
MOON'S COMIN' UP.
THAT WILEY OLD RASCAL.
HI, GUYS!
WHAT'S NEW TONIGHT, MOON?
OH... NOTHIN'.
JUST GOT MY COPERNICUS CRATER PIERCED. NO BIGGIE.
GOSH. MOON RULES. ALWAYS UP TO SOMETHING.
IS THE SUN STILL COOLER THAN ME? IF SO, HOW?
WHAT'S HIS DEAL?
J. BURRELLO 2023

OH. HELLO, FRIENDS.
BATH-TUB BENNY
POP
SADLY, EVEN GREAT BATHS MUST COME TO AN END.
GLUG
GLUG
GLUG
CUZ IF THEY DIDN'T...
SLUSH
...WOULD WE EVEN APPRECIATE THEM WHEN THEY HAPPENED?
SLOSH
I'D LIKE TO THINK I STILL WOULD
BLUB
GLUG
BUT JUST IN CASE...
SLORSH
BLUB
GLUG
BLUB
I'LL JUST ACCEPT THE TEMPORARY.
AND SEE WHAT THE NEXT PHASE OF LIFE HAS TO OFFER.
BLUB
SQUEAK
GURGLE

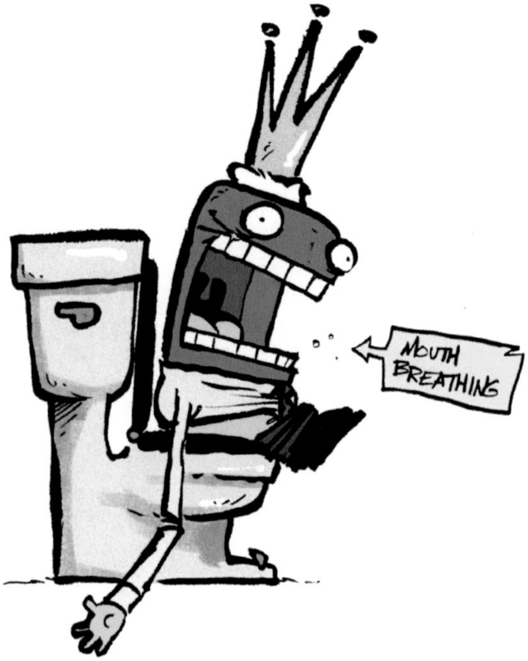
MOUTH BREATHING

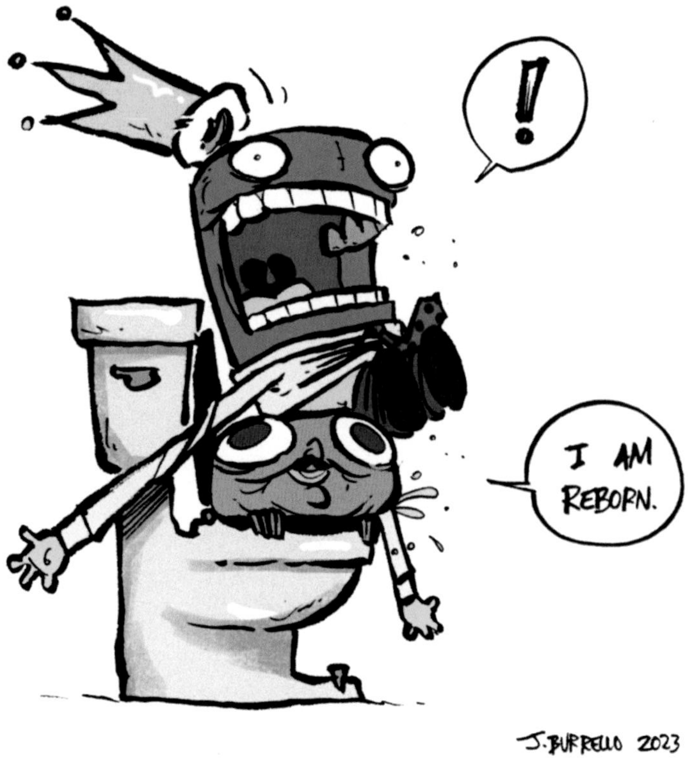
!
I AM REBORN.

J. BURRELLO 2023

Fin

OTHER BOOKS

Woolly the Big Cow

Straight from the Pit of Hell

Toddspeed

Propaganda

Year of the Bat

The Book of Barb

COLLABS

Eyrbyggja Saga: a Tale from Old Iceland

Werewolves Don't Celebrate Hanukkah

The Orc Who Saved Christmas

Dragons Don't Celebrate Passover

Handcrafted plushies of Blinky, Sal, and Todd lurk at TeamManticore.com.

If you dig Haunted Safari, check out my other comic, **Barb**. It's about a barbarian girl and her friends as they hack their way through perilous situations and perilouser monsters.

Follow the adventures of **BARB** on Webtoon!

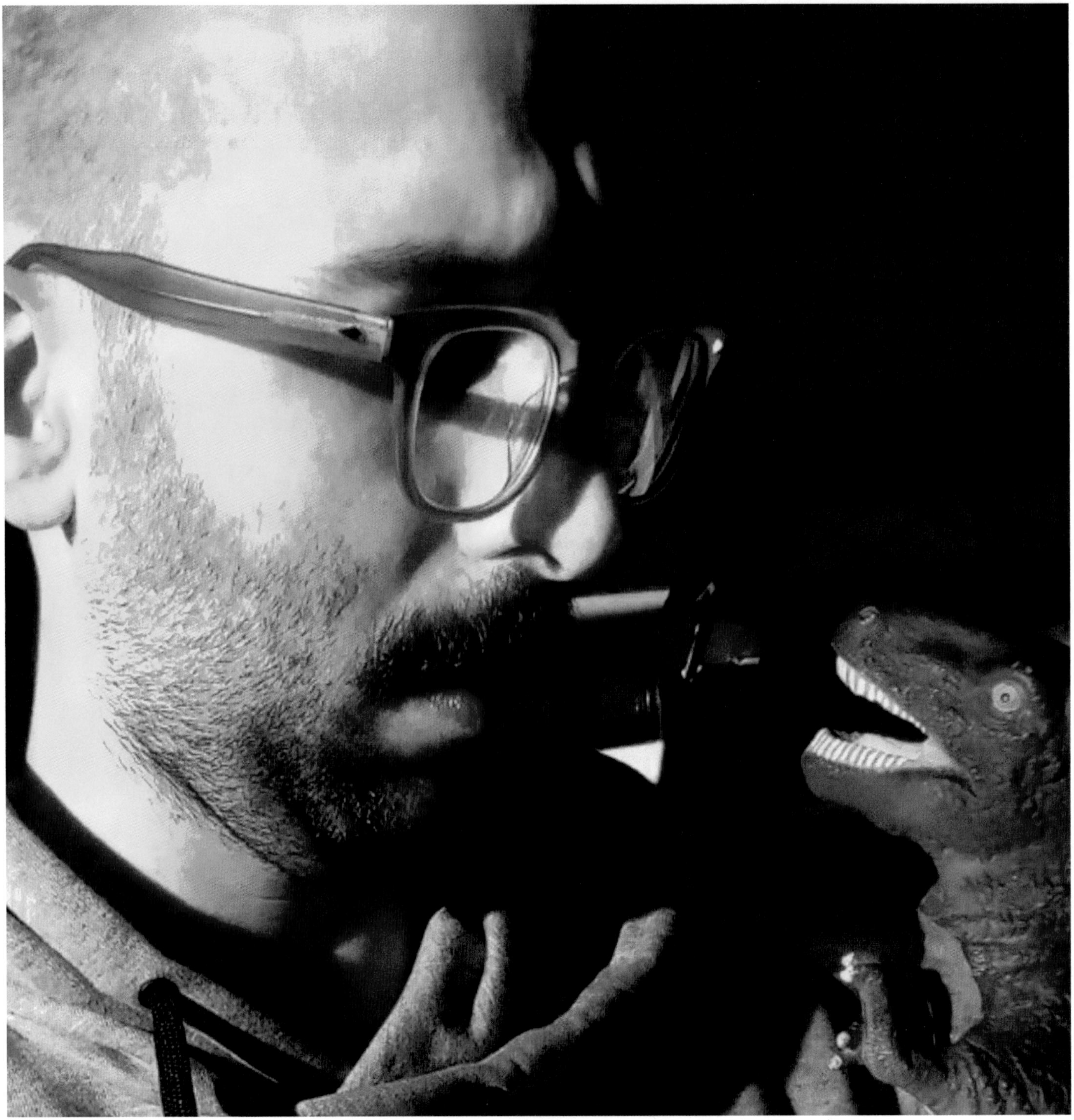

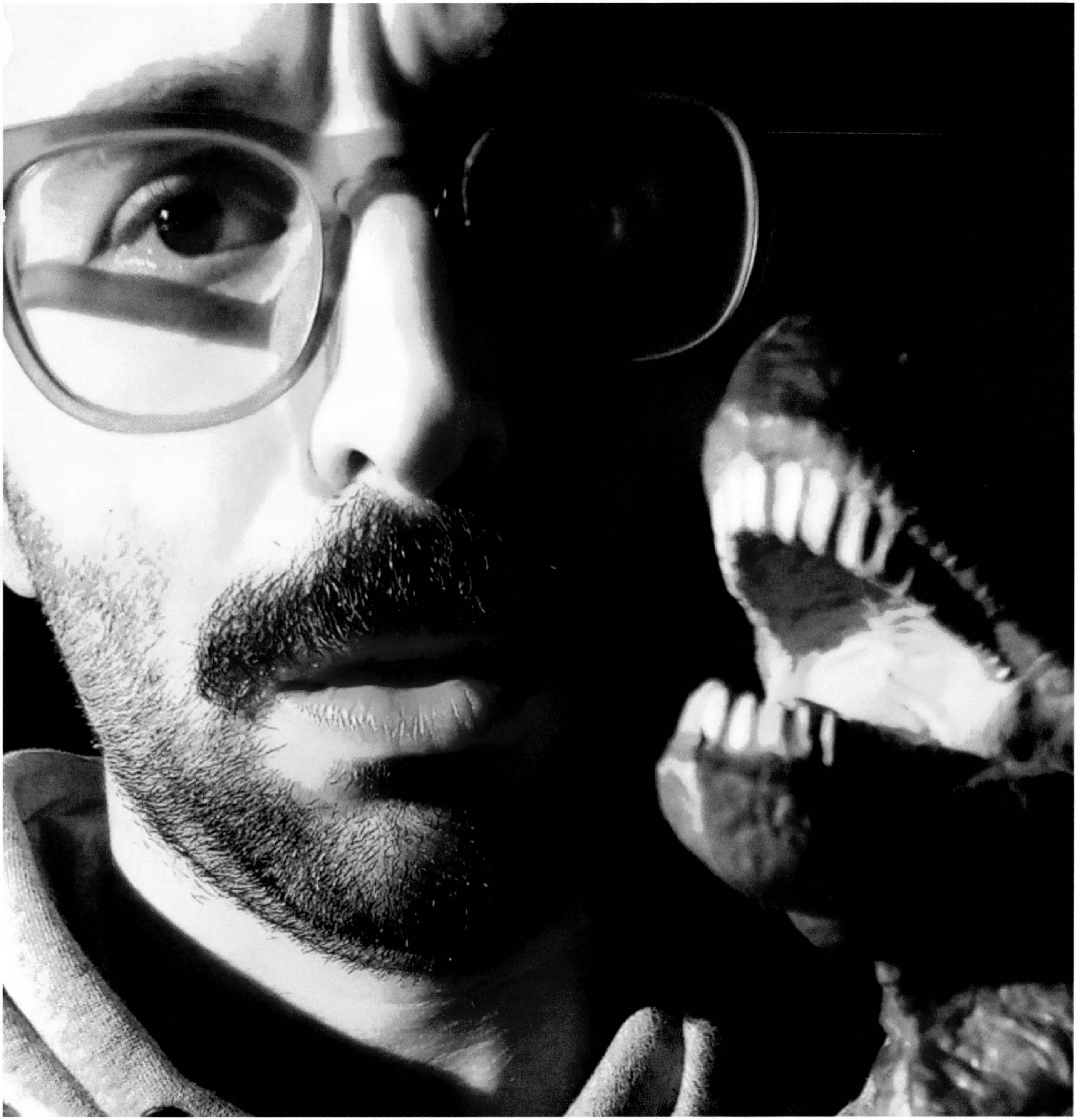

This has been a test of the Emergency Comic System. If this had been an actual emergency, you would have been instructed to climb into your bathtub with all of your clothes on (probably even layer up a bit with a coat or scarf, what have you), let the hot water run until it floods the downstairs, contact a notary public, ask them what it is they do exactly when they're not stamping papers, make a quick sketch of your favorite dinosaur, and await

further instruction.

Made in the USA
Columbia, SC
15 April 2023

14948312R00058